Making
WOODEN
CHESS SETS

Making
WOODEN
CHESS SETS

15 One-of-a-Kind Projects for the Scroll Saw

Jim Kape

FOX CHAPEL
PUBLISHING

Making Wooden Chess Sets is an original work, first published in 2010 by Fox Chapel Publishing Company, Inc. The patterns contained herein are copyrighted by the author. Readers may make copies of these patterns for personal use. The patterns themselves, however, are not to be duplicated for resale or distribution under any circumstances. Any such copying is a violation of copyright law.

ISBN 978-1-56523-457-4

Library of Congress Cataloging-in-Publication Data

Kape, Jim.
 Making wooden chess sets : 15 one-of-a-kind projects for the scroll saw / by Jim Kape.
     p. cm.
 Includes bibliographical references and index.
 ISBN 978-1-56523-457-4 (alk. paper)
 1. Chessmen. 2. Chess sets. 3. Woodwork--Patterns. 4. Jig saws. I. Title.
 TT896.55.K37 2010
 684'.08--dc22
                        2010020407

To learn more about the other great books from Fox Chapel Publishing, or to find a retailer near you, call toll-free 800-457-9112 or visit us at *www.FoxChapelPublishing.com*.

Note to Authors: We are always looking for talented authors to write new books in our area of woodworking, design, and related crafts. Please send a brief letter describing your idea to Acquisition Editor, 1970 Broad Street, East Petersburg, PA 17520.

Printed in China
First printing: December 2010

Dedication

This book is dedicated to my father. He passed

away before he could see the things I'm most

proud of in my life: my children and my own

legacy. This book and the work involved in putting

it together are a labor of love that he would have

been proud of. I love you Dad.

Contents

About this Book

You'll take a tour through the world and history when you make one of these chess sets. No matter what your interest, there is a unique chess design here for you. Step-by-step instructions are included for the Classic Set, as well as a chessboard, simple storage box, travel chess set, and vertical chess set. The complete pattern appendix contains every pattern you need to make the projects in this book—thanks to multiple patterns of the pieces that require them, you'll need to copy only three pages to make each set.

Classic: A classic chess set for those who prefer the traditional look. Page 25.

King Henry VIII: A rotund design with nice heft. Page 40.

Trojan: A Greek-inspired set that will transport your chessboard to the Mediterranean. Page 43.

Paris: Explore the romantic motifs of Paris in this miniature monument to France's handsome capital. Page 52.

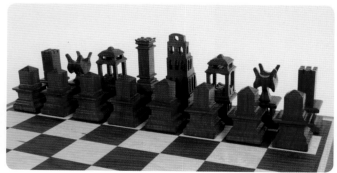

Roman Glory: Recall the Roman history you learned in school while battling gladiator-style on the chessboard. Page 55.

Neo-Classic: A twist on the classic chess set that features curves and points. Page 34.

Neo-Classic II: A curvy, soft-cornered alternative design. Page 37.

Peter the Great: An epic design that invokes the beautiful historic architecture of Russia. Page 46.

Canterbury: A bevy of interior cuts highlights the grandness of this English-inspired set. Page 49.

San Francisco: This creative design represents San Francisco's most notable landmarks in chess form—including the streetcar. Page 58.

Venice: A regal design focusing on Venice's diverse architectural wonders. Page 61.

Introduction

The Henry VIII set in the Castle at Ashley Manor, Chandler, Arizona.

Imagine yourself in my shoes for a moment. It was winter in Arizona, a crisp 65° outside. The grass was green and the desert was resting before bursting forth in another blast-furnace summer. I had just finished a beautiful cherry jewelry box as a Christmas present for my niece, and it came out even better than imagined. After this success, my passion for woodworking was growing exponentially. I was at a crossroads: what was going to be the next project? Something in the back of my mind whispered "chess set." As I puzzled it over, I realized it would be something elegant and refined. This was something I had wanted to build since high school, when a friend of mine brought one home from wood shop.

Building the board was fairly easy. There were multiple plans online, so I ordered the lumber. I selected maple and walnut. This would turn out to be a great combination for a chessboard. The woods have similar characteristics, and contrast each other very well. I built the board using a cheap portable table saw, wood glue, and clamps. After sanding and finishing, it looked fantastic.

I had a picture in my mind of what the pieces should look like, but no idea how to bring them to life. I glued some scrap walnut and maple together to make a composite chess piece. My first attempt was to sand them into shape with a bench belt sander. I made a lot of sawdust, but no chess pieces. Then I pulled out my old rotary tool and tried to power carve them. Again, I made a big mess, but no chess pieces. I then thought it might be easier to just carve them by hand. I didn't make a big mess this time, but it didn't take long for me to figure out that maple and walnut are hard to carve by hand. I was still without any chess pieces. I was stumped. I knew I could use a lathe to turn the pieces, but I had never used a lathe and did not have the funds to invest in one. I then thought of a scroll saw. I had had one many years before, but had very little success with it. In reading online, I figured out the mistakes I had made with my first saw, so I decided to invest in another one. Luckily, I found a scroll saw online for $30.

Next I had to figure out the patterns for the pieces. After about 3 hours of intense work on the computer, I had a design. This design would evolve into the Classic Set that is in this book. I took that pattern and cut my first piece.

The piece was rough, but came out much better than I had anticipated. So I kept designing and building. I designed several chess pieces that would never see the light of day because the design was so bad. Some of the designs turned out very well and are also found in this book. As I grew more comfortable with designing, I became more daring in my designs, including inside cuts, complex curves, different bases, and many other things.

The first chess piece cut by the author.

I shared one design, based on the Notre Dame Cathedral in Paris, with a scroll saw friend, and he turned that into an award-winning chess set. It took prizes in both his county and state fairs. I took that same design and entered it in a local woodworking competition and came away with a blue ribbon. I was hooked. I would go to sleep thinking about designs, draw them during the day, and cut them in the evening.

This book has been a labor of love. It has taken my sawdust therapy and turned it into something I hope will last and be useful for many years to come. This book has been put together to provide you, the reader, with designs, descriptions, pictures, and ideas. For every woodworker I've ever met, that's enough to get the juices flowing. If you are just starting out, take your time and think through what you are going to do. If you are unsure, find an online forum and ask questions. There is not a woodworker out there who has not needed a question answered. If you are an experienced craftsman, you probably have jumped ahead to the designs and changed them already. I hope I've provided enough food for thought for every person who picks up this book. I hope you enjoy building your chess set or sets as much as I have putting this together.

Happy cutting!

Jim Kape

Jim Kape

About Chess

Why are we so drawn to this game? I think it has something to do with the history of chess. It is a game that blended life in the middle ages and the Renaissance into a board game of infinite possibilities that all fit on 64 little colored squares. The game is elegant, as are the sets. Owners of fine chess sets get an implied 20 extra IQ points for having one around, even if the only player is the house cat.

History of Chess

The game can be traced back to a sixth century game in India. This game featured the four major pieces of a then-modern army: the infantry, cavalry, elephant, and chariot. These have turned into the pawn, knight, bishop, and rook, respectively. The game found its way to Europe via traders, merchants, and conquerors from the east starting in the ninth century. The game further evolved until around 1475, when most of the rules we use today were adopted. Strategy and tactics for the game were first published in the fifteenth century and have continued through the present day.

The first modern chess tournament was held in 1851 in London, and was won by German player Adolf Anderssen. This was the beginning of the game as a sport. Individual games and players were featured in newspaper columns and periodicals dedicated to the game. In 1849, Howard Staunton, considered the best player in the world, wrote about a chess set designed by Nathaniel Cook and manufactured by Jaques of London. In this article, he praised the design for being easily identifiable and sturdy. Staunton lent his name to the set and actually signed the box for each set that left the factory. This is the basic chess set we know today.

San Francisco chess set.

Rules of the Game

For a game to not only survive, but thrive, for as long as chess has in the same basic form, you would think the rules would need to be simple and obvious. That is not necessarily the case. A game of chess is a ballet of deep thought in which each player seeks to place the other in a position of jeopardy from which he or she cannot escape. The game involves strategy and tactics, thinking many moves ahead, trickery, bluffs, attack, and defense. Chess is one of the world's most popular games, transcending language, race, and nationality.

This is a very rudimentary set of rules, and much more complete descriptions and diagrams for the game are found online and in books. If chess gets in your blood and you can't get enough of it, check your local community for chess clubs and competitions.

The board

The board the game is played on is 64 squares, alternating in light and dark colors. The squares are arranged in an 8-by-8 grid. Traditionally, the game is begun with a light square on each player's right hand.

The players

There are two players in a game of chess—one person using the light-colored pieces, the other using the dark-colored pieces. The player using the light-colored pieces is called White, while the player using the dark-colored pieces is called Black.

The pieces

There are six different pieces in a chess set: the king, queen, bishop, knight, rook, and pawn.

- **King:** Taking this piece is the objective for each player. While it is usually the largest piece on the board, it is not the most powerful, and is limited to moving a single square in any direction.

- **Queen:** This is the most powerful piece on the board for each player. The queen is able to move in any single direction as far as possible, without jumping over any pieces.

- **Bishop:** There are two bishops per side. Each player has a bishop that starts the game on a light square and another on a dark square. Since the bishop moves only diagonally, the light bishop will rest only on light-colored squares, and the dark bishop will rest only on dark-colored squares. This piece also needs a clear lane of movement and cannot jump other pieces. Each bishop can move multiple squares in a single direction per turn.

- **Knight:** Unlike the other pieces on the board, the knight does not move in a straight line, and can jump over other pieces. The knight's move is two squares vertically or horizontally, and one square to the side. The move will look like a large letter *L* every time. Each player starts the game with two knights.

Paris chess set.

Rook: This castle piece moves in a straight line horizontally or vertically as far as possible without jumping other pieces. It can also move in conjunction with the king in what is called *castling*. This is moving the king toward the rook two squares, and putting the rook on the adjoining square on the opposite side of the king. Each player also begins the game with two rooks.

Pawn: Seemingly the least powerful pieces on the board, the pawns are very important. Their move is one or two squares forward on the first move, and one move forward thereafter. If the pawn is attacking another piece, it will take the piece one diagonal square forward in either direction. If a player's pawn moves to the end row of the board, it can be exchanged for any other piece, usually a queen. There are eight pawns for each side.

Starting positions

The pieces start the game at the two base rows for each player. The first row for white will have the rooks on either end, the knights inside the rooks, and the bishops inside the knights. The king takes the right hand of the last two squares on the base row, with the queen taking the other. The second row is filled with the eight pawns. For black, the only difference is the order of the king and queen. The black king faces the white king directly, and so will take the left square of the two left after placing the rooks, knights, and bishops on the board. A good way to remember this is that the queen always starts on a square of her own color.

Playing the game

White begins the game with the first move, and the two players alternate play with one move per turn. When the king is in jeopardy, known as *check*, it must be rescued. This is accomplished by moving the king out of check, moving a piece in the way of the attacking piece, or taking the attacking piece.

Venice chess set at the Castle at Ashley Manor, Chandler, Arizona.

Chapter *1*

Getting Started

Getting a new book and seeing all the fantastic designs might make you want to get busy making sawdust. But as with the new bicycle on Christmas morning, it works out much better if you take the time to read the fine print. Read on to find out about safety, the tools and materials you'll use in these projects, and information about cutting and finishing.

Did you know?

The scroll saw today comes from more than 400 years of evolution. In the 1500s, some unknown person—probably a clock-maker—figured out how to make fine metal blades, and a Parisian named Boulle invented a U-shaped frame to put the blade on. The handheld version of the scroll saw was born.

Safety

Please note: Some of the pictures in this book show the author using tools without safety guards, or with fingers very close to the blade. This is done to illustrate the technique, not to illustrate how to use tools without safety items. Each cut was planned with consideration for placement of hands and body and what would happen if anything unplanned happened with the power tool.

Manuals

The first guideline for safety is to read the manual for each power tool. The manual is the best place to find the safety aspects of each tool, and how to use the tools properly. Replacement manuals or online versions can be found on the Internet, so even second- and third-hand power tools can be used safely.

Read and save the manuals for your power tools.

Preparations

The second guideline for safety is to not turn the power on until you are ready. This is a very broad statement. It means the tool is set up, the cutting stock is ready, the work area is clean and clear, and you've taken care of any foreseeable distractions that could occur while you're running the tool.

The pictures in this book were taken in my garage over the course of several months. There were many times when I packed up for the day because kids were playing nearby. It is hard enough concentrating on my own safety, but with kids around, the level of risk just got too high. It is much better to sacrifice the rest of the daylight and start again tomorrow, than to sacrifice a finger.

Environment

The third guideline for safety is to have a safe work environment. If the floor is full of dust and scrap, take a moment and sweep it up. If the bench is four layers deep in tools, take a few minutes to clean them up and put them away. If the next step generates dust or spray, use a particulate mask. If the next task can generate wood chips, use safety glasses or a face shield. Don't underestimate the power of a small wooden chip or dust. Both can seriously injure even the strongest person.

Pay attention to the consumable items being used. This means the wood being cut, finishes, cleaning compounds, waxes, anything used and possibly thrown away. Most of this is toxic to some greater or lesser degree. Exposure to sawdust can cause people to develop allergies, which could limit the enjoyment they get out of woodworking. Inhaling the spray from the finish can lead to diminished breathing capacity or asthma. So respect the items being used, understand the effect they may have, and take the precautions necessary to reduce or eliminate the exposures.

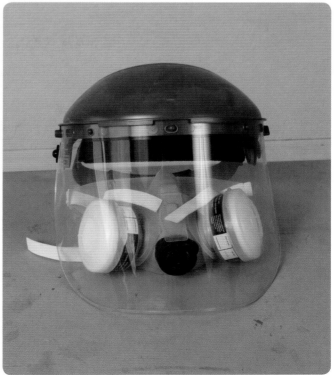

Wearing a face shield and respirator while creating the projects in this book will help you to prevent many easily avoided health problems.

Tools

There are a number of tools used to create the items in this book. The two used the most are the scroll saw and table saw. All of the tools are listed below along with their use.

- **Scroll saw:** Cuts chess pieces, fretwork, box joints, and dividers.
- **Table saw:** Sizes cutting stock for chess pieces and other structural pieces.
- **Miter saw:** Cuts miters for borders, sizes smaller pieces, and separates chess piece blanks via a flush cut on the bottom.
- **Drill press:** Creates holes that are perfectly perpendicular to the wood being drilled. Can also be used to cut holes at a consistent depth.
- **Twist drill bits:** The normal drill bit everyone recognizes. Used for countersinking screw heads.
- **Brad-point drill bits:** Very accurate drill bit that has the least tendency to wander. Recommended for all starting holes for inside cuts.
- **Forstner drill bits:** Drills large flat-bottomed holes. Used for drilling magnet or weight holes in the bottom of chess pieces or shelves.
- **Belt sander:** Removes wood and glue quickly from items that have been glued together. Used mostly to clean up a surface quickly.
- **Random orbit sander:** Removes tool marks and is used to get a progressively smoother finish on wood.
- **Sanding block:** Comes in very handy when it's too awkward to use a power sanding tool.

Top to bottom: Forstner drill bit, brad-point drill bit, twist drill bit.

- **Emery board:** Invaluable for cleaning up the inside cuts for chess pieces and fretwork.
- **Chisels:** Clean up boxes after they've been cut apart, and create recesses for hinges.
- **Router:** Creates smooth edges and corners.
- **Router table:** A flat surface to which a router is attached, allowing the operator to move the piece rather than the tool.
- **Air compressor:** Compresses air for use in air tools.
- **Brad nailer:** Attaches a border to a base. This makes a much stronger joint when used with glue.
- **Sprayer:** Applies polyurethane or lacquer finishes.
- **Blower:** Cleans sawdust out of pieces.
- **Gloves:** Protect the hands from chemicals or glue.
- **Clamps:** Keep a constant pressure on any joint being glued.
- **Shop vacuum:** Cleans up the inevitable dust and dirt.
- **Reversible drill:** Creates pilot holes for screws.
- **Screwdrivers:** Drive screws into the wood.
- **Pencil:** Marks wood for cutting guides or assembly guides.
- **Ruler:** A shorter metal ruler is used for accurate measures, and a longer metal ruler is used for an assembly guide.
- **Carpenter's square:** Verifies absolute square for larger assemblies and jigs.
- **Combination square:** Verifies square and draws a perpendicular line.

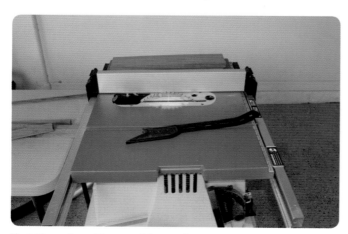

The table saw is used in many of these projects.

Consumable Materials

These are items used during the course of assembly that are consumed by the project.

- **Wood glue:** Joins two pieces of wood together.
- **CA (Cyanoacrylate) glue:** Creates an almost instant bond between almost any surfaces.
- **Waterproof wood glue:** Joins two pieces of wood. This glue has slightly different long-term characteristics than normal wood glue.
- **Spray adhesive:** Attaches patterns to the chess piece cutting stock, and felt to the bottom of the chess pieces.
- **Blue painter's tape:** Used on all pieces that are scrolled. Provides an easy-to-remove surface between the pattern and the wood. The adhesive also provides a lubricant to the scroll saw blade during cutting.
- **Mineral spirits:** Cleans pieces and removes accidental applications of flocking adhesive.
- **Danish oil:** A long-lasting, oil-based wood finish.
- **Polyurethane spray:** A long-lasting and hard-wearing wood finish.
- **Lead shot, pennies, or tungsten putty:** Weights the chess pieces.
- **Epoxy:** Very strong and long-lasting adhesive. Used to attach weights to chess pieces.
- **Wood putty:** Fills in gaps left during the assembly of wooden pieces.

Cutting Stock

There are a couple of considerations for cutting stock. The first is the ease of cutting a piece that will be 1½" (38mm) thick. Some woods just are not well-suited for this. Rosewood and purpleheart come to mind as woods that would be beautiful, but are almost impossible to use for compound cutting because of their characteristics.

The second consideration is grain and finished beauty. The chess pieces have some interesting curves and lines that will complement unique grain in wood. Zebrawood, mahogany, maple, walnut, and sapele are good examples of wood that will surprise you with hidden beauty when you finish them.

The final consideration is thickness. For the examples in the book, the wood used was purchased at 8/4 (eight quarters, or about 2" [51mm]) thick. The lumber is then cut down to size on a table saw. An alternate approach is to get 4/4 (four quarter) lumber and glue it together to create the thickness necessary. My personal preference is the 8/4 wood, but a few pieces shown in this book were done with glued-up wood.

As a general rule, 55" (1.4m) of 1½" by 1½" (38mm by 38mm) wood (five 11" [279mm] sticks) will provide enough stock for an entire chess set, with some extra left over for rework. Care must be taken to put the patterns on the lumber before cutting the individual pieces so the lumber can be used in the most efficient manner.

Left to right, ½" (13mm) maple, 4/4 maple, 1½" x 1½" (38mm x 38mm) wenge, 1½" x 1½" (38mm x 38mm) padauk, 1½" x 1½" (38mm x 38mm) spalted maple, 1½" x 1½" (38mm x 38mm) Spanish cedar (note glue line), 8/4 walnut.

Design

How does design fit in? The design is the recipe for the set. It gives guidelines and provides some confidence to the craftsman building it. Designing a compound-cut piece takes patience and an understanding of how a complimentary cut (one at 90° to the first cut) will affect the design. For example, take a water tower. It's a simple design, and because it's common, almost everyone knows what it looks like.

If we want to add the pipe in the middle for the water to flow down, we end up with an extra two legs (see photo at right).

What happened? The answer is the shadow effect. Material is taken away from the object in the first cut. Anything that is under the area to be saved will be in the final product unless removed by the complimentary cut. In this example the complimentary cut has to leave material for the legs. The middle outside legs are shadowed by both sides of the cut, and therefore remain in the end result. Unless the designer is using a complex 3-D modeling computer program, or can imagine the end result in his or her head, there will be surprises like this anytime inside cuts are used.

The shadow effect limits compound design in other areas as well. There is no way to cut convex or concave shapes except for simple ones that have a vertical axis. Take the hand, pictured at right, as an example. There is no way to hollow out the palm and make it seem more lifelike unless we carve the piece after it is scrolled. So liberties are often taken with the designs to keep them structurally sound as well as aesthetically pleasing.

Compound-cut water tower.

Unintentional extra legs appear on the sides when adding the center downpipe.

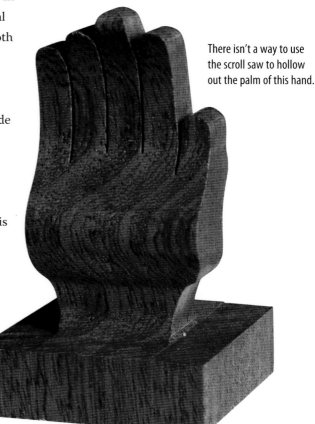
There isn't a way to use the scroll saw to hollow out the palm of this hand.

20

Cutting Techniques

Cutting stock 1½" (38mm) thick is very different from cutting stock that is ¼" (6mm) thick. The feed rate will be significantly slower, but more heat is generated, and unless special care is taken to keep any sideways pressure off the blade, the blade can bow and ruin a piece. So the general guidelines are to use the correct blade (see below), go slow, use more thumb as feed pressure than finger, and if you smell something getting hot, stop. Scorching pieces is a side effect of too much pressure or using the wrong blade.

Using a jig (page 29) also increases the odds of success. The jig adds more weight and size to the piece being cut, and provides more stability. It does make cutting a little slower, as you have to set up the jig for every cut, but the benefits outweigh the cost of time. See the pattern for the jig on page 127.

There are also three specific cutting techniques that will save time and frustration.

270° technique

It sounds high tech, but it is just taking the long way on outside corners. For example, take a look at the illustrations at right. The black arrows show the cutting direction.

The simple approach would be to cut the corner by making a sharp turn at the point (center). While this is indeed simple, it also will provide a less-than-sharp edge, and on many woods, will scorch the inside of the cut with the increased heat from the blade.

The way to get around both problems is to instead take the long way around and come at the new face of the cut from outside, utilizing the waste portion of the wood being cut. Some of the pieces will need so many cuts like this, it will appear that toothpicks are being cut instead of chess pieces, if judged by the scrap wood on the floor of the shop. However, the resulting chess piece will have nice sharp, clean, scorch-free corners.

Begin by cutting up the outside edge of the piece.

Chess Piece Being Cut

You could try to make an abrupt right angle to create the corner, but you'll likely run into some issues.

Chess Piece Being Cut

A better option is to cut a small loop in the waste wood and come back at the next edge from straight on.

Chess Piece Being Cut

Inside corner milling technique

The inside corner milling technique is used when an inside corner needs to be cut.

Take a look at the illustration at right. There is an inside cut coming up. The simple method of cutting this corner would be to simply turn the piece and continue (center).

But if we cut it this way, we will have a less-than-sharp corner, and create a risk that the blade will bow if any side pressure is put on the piece during the turn. So to sharpen up the corner and make the turn less risky, cut up to the end of the first line, back up, and start to mill off some room in the inside of the elbow (bottom right). When there is enough room to turn the piece and get the blade flush, start cutting in the new direction.

Smooth landing technique

The smooth landing technique deals with cutting corners in internal areas. The first step is creating a blade entry hole. Patterns with doorways and windows are perfect to use this technique on. In the diagram below, the circle is the hole that has been drilled. The two arrows show two cuts coming out of the hole and curving into the corner (the smooth landing). This provides a sharp corner, and when the piece of waste is removed, the blade can be put flush against the cut and continued around the rest of the pattern.

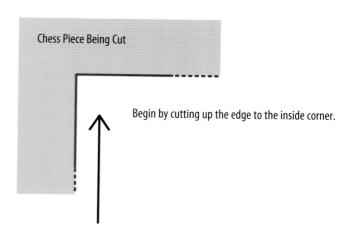

Begin by cutting up the edge to the inside corner.

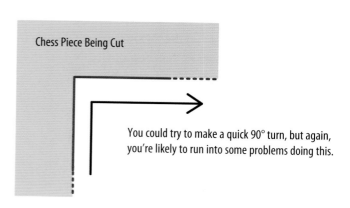

You could try to make a quick 90° turn, but again, you're likely to run into some problems doing this.

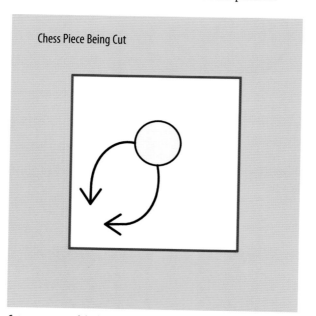

Cut a curve out of the blade entry hole to swoop into the interior corner.

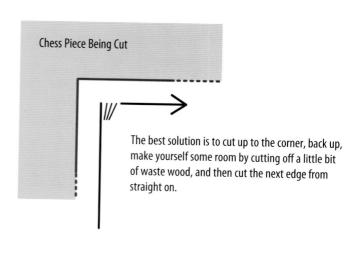

The best solution is to cut up to the corner, back up, make yourself some room by cutting off a little bit of waste wood, and then cut the next edge from straight on.

The correct blade

What is the correct blade to use? For cutting chess pieces, the correct blade is a larger blade, a #5 or #7, with an aggressive tooth pattern. A number of different blades fit this description, and finding the right one for you requires trial and error. Get some samples of different blades and try them. Cut a chess piece and see what the result is. You will find that there is a blade that works best for you, your saw, and the lumber you are cutting.

Finishing

Finishing not only protects the project, but intensifies the luster and grain of the wood. A proper finish can take a great project and make it extraordinary. When finishing chess sets, we are protecting them from grime and wear during use, but also from moisture.

Before the finish can be applied, make sure all the necessary construction and assembly steps have been completed. If the design calls for embedded magnets, make sure the magnets have been glued inside the piece and the resultant hole has been filled with wood putty. If the design calls for weights, be sure to add the weights, and glue them in place, and as with the magnets, be sure to fill in the hole with wood putty. The final step before applying the finish is to get rid of any fuzzies on the edges of the chess pieces. This is a normal by-product of scrolling, and will be present to some degree in almost any cut. There are ways to minimize the presence of the fuzzies, but no way to eliminate them. A regular emery board is the most effective way to take care of this. Just rub the board along the edge with the fuzzies and they come off easily. Look at the edges and especially at the inside cuts. That's where the fuzzies seem to love to hide.

The next step is to decide on the finish to be used. In this book, I've used two finishes: Danish oil and spray polyurethane.

Danish oil

For the chess pieces, immerse the pieces in a tray partially filled with oil to get all of the exposed surfaces covered. This method is particularly effective with pieces that have inside cuts. I use a small tray, immerse the pieces, and then set them upright on a shop rag. Let them dry for about half an hour and dunk them again. Then use a combination of compressed air and a clean dry shop rag to remove all the leftover oil. The piece will need overnight to cure, but will have a warm, satin smooth finish in the morning.

For chessboards or boxes, wiping the oil on with a shop rag is the best method. In both cases, read the manufacturer's instructions on the oil container.

Spray polyurethane

Spray finish is the easiest to use. For most chess pieces, I use a spray lacquer I buy from a local home improvement store. The lacquer is pre-mixed and is almost foolproof. Just use light coats and be sure to get all the surfaces.

Felt

Once the piece has the finish on it, the final step is to add felt to the bottom of the piece. This was a standard part of the Staunton chess sets, and the goal was to make the pieces seem to float above the board. There are a number of options for felt, from press-apply felt to craft felt to felt fabric. The brown felt used on the chessboard and the chess pieces shown in this book was bought by the yard at a local fabric store, and glued to the pieces with spray adhesive.

23

Venice chess set at the Castle at Ashley Manor, Chandler, Arizona.

2 The Chess Sets

In this section, all of the designs for the individual pieces are showcased with full-color pictures, cutting notes, comments on the wood used, and other information about the design itself. Read through the step-by-step instructions for cutting the Classic set, select your favorite chess set, and get scrolling!

Did you know?

An Italian Dominican Monk, Jacobus de Cessolis, wrote a book titled *Liber de moribus hominum et officiis nobilium sive super ludo scacchorum*, which is translated to *Book of the Customs of Men and the Duties of Nobles* or the *Book of Chess*, around the year 1300. This was one of the first books translated into English.

Classic Chess Set

Wood Notes

In this example, I used aromatic cedar and alder. Aromatic cedar is extremely easy to cut—it does not scorch or sear easily, and is very soft. Beware of the constant changing grain in the wood. It will produce some weak spots that you may need to reinforce with some CA glue. Alder is also very easy to cut. It does not scorch or sear easily, and has a tight strong grain. Recommended woods for a beginner include alder, maple, walnut, or basswood. Because of the unpredictability of aromatic cedar, I would not recommend it until you have become comfortable cutting compound pieces.

This was my first design, and to be honest, one of the most fun. Learning how to cut these pieces and how to design them at the same time was challenging, but rewarding. The design of the Classic Chess Set takes inspiration from the de facto standard in chess set design—the Staunton Chess Set. This design was set forth in 1849 by Nathaniel Cook and publicly endorsed by Howard Staunton, the best chess player in the world at the time. The Staunton design was the first to use crowns for the king and queen and a cross pattée on top of the king. The bishop is designed to look like a stylized mitre cap of the clergy. The knight is the rampant horse, the rook the castle battlements, and the pawn a simple piece with a ball on top.

The ribbed feet and collars offer a bit of a challenge. Take your time and mill off enough room to turn around at the inside of the rib. For the headpiece of the queen and the cross of the king, make sure to use the 270° cutting technique (see page 21) to get good crisp edges. Take your time—these are big pieces and cutting through thick stock is not by any means quick. In the end, you will have a chess set you can be proud of for many years to come. Patterns for the Classic Chess Set are on pages 90–92.

King

The king stands tall at 4⅜" (111mm). The base is a standard block that transitions into two ribs and then to the narrow waist. The collar is three ribs, with the centermost brought farther out from the other two. The head is large and round, with a slight, flat top and a large cross. The design is symmetrical, with the exception of the cross at the top. Cut the side with the cross first, as this provides more room for potential error on the other side.

Queen

The queen is also a very tall piece at 4" (102mm) tall. She uses the same base, waist, and collar the king uses, just slightly shorter. The head is large with a wide crown. When cutting this crown, be sure to cut beyond the design on the sharp edges and circle around to start the next line. See the "Getting Started" section (page 21) about the 270° technique.

Bishop

The bishop stands 3⅛" (79mm) tall, utilizing the same style of base and waist as the king and queen, just shorter. The collar is three ribbed, but all three ribs are the same size. The miter hat with an angled cutout stays faithful to the Staunton design.

Knight

The knight was the most problematic of the designs. To get a horsehead in proportions close to an actual horse, using compound cutting techniques, is nearly impossible. This is a compromise, with the design based on a horse with the head stately and regal, not rampant as in the Staunton design. The waist is shortened dramatically to allow room for the large head.

Rook

The rook stands 2¹¹⁄₁₆" (68mm) tall. It uses the same base and waist as the rest of the pieces, but again, shorter than the rest. The collar is a single rib that transitions into the castle battlements that are typical of the Staunton design. This design has three crenelations on each side, which provides a bit more balance than just two. When cutting the top, again use the 270° technique (page 21).

Pawn

This piece stands 2⅛" (54mm) tall, and uses the same base and waist design as the other pieces. The single collar rib transitions into a round ball top, again, consistent with the Staunton design. These pieces are a joy to cut—they go quickly and each piece will have a unique ball due to how the grain of the wood is cut.

Making the Classic Chess Set

Materials and Tools

Tools
- Scroll saw
- Compound cutting jig (page 127)
- Table saw
- Miter saw (optional)
- 200-grit sandpaper
- Emery board
- Drill press
- ⅞" (22mm) Forstner drill bit
- Putty knife
- Scissors

Materials
- 55" (1.4m) of 1½" x 1½" (38mm x 38mm) lumber per single 16-piece set (you will need double to make both the white and black sides)
- 2" (51mm)-wide blue painter's tape
- Spray adhesive
- Copied patterns from pages 90–92 for 1 king, 1 queen, 2 bishops, 2 knights, 2 rooks, and 8 pawns (you will need double to make both the white and black sides)
- About 3 pounds (1.3kg) of lead shot, pennies, or tungsten putty
- Wood putty
- About 1 square-foot felt
- 30-minute epoxy
- Oil or polyurethane finish

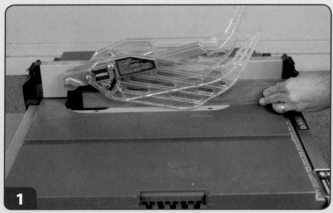

1 **Cut the stock.** The first step is to get the cutting stock to the 1½" x 1½" (38mm x 38mm) dimensions. A table saw is the easiest way. I normally start with 8/4 (eight quarter or 2" [51mm]-thick lumber. But if 8/4 lumber is hard to come by, standard 4/4 glued together works fine.

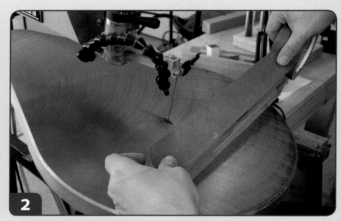

2 **Apply tape.** Once the lumber is dimensioned, cover all sides with blue painter's tape. This provides a good surface for the pattern to be attached, but also provides some important lubrication to the scroll saw blade as the piece is cut.

3 **Prepare patterns.** Copy or print the patterns (from pages 90–91) on normal copy paper and then cut them out. Don't cut across the dashed line that shows where the crease will go on the two-sided pattern.

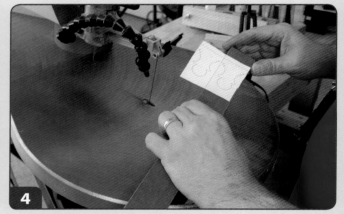

4 **Apply patterns.** Spray the back of the pattern with spray adhesive. Line up the dashed line with the corner of the stock. Both the top and the bottom should perfectly align with the edge of the stock. Firmly attach both sides, and continue until all patterns are attached.

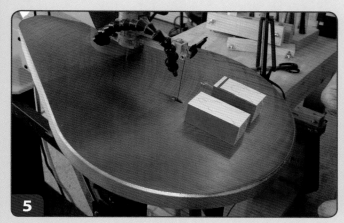

5

Separate pieces. Separate the individual pieces by cutting across the bottom of the base. This can be done on the scroll saw, but a quicker and more consistent method is to use a miter saw.

6

Drill weight holes. According to the Staunton standard, the pieces should be weighted. You'll need to drill a ⅞" (22mm) hole ½" (13mm) deep in the base of each chess piece. To find the center, draw a line from opposing corners on the bottom. Use the intersection as the drill point. Make a simple jig (below) to hold the piece stable while drilling.

7

Prepare compound cutting jig. To cut the individual pieces, use a compound cutting jig (right). Put two pieces in the jig and tighten. Make sure the jig is stable by trying to wiggle it side to side. If wiggles, loosen one bolt at a time, press the jig and piece flat into the table, and retighten.

Compound Cutting Jig

This little helper is as important as the scroll saw for getting the chess sets cut. Each jig takes two pieces cut to the pattern shown here. Cut the jig from scrap stock that is 4/4. After cutting the two sides to the jig, turn the pieces so the holes are horizontal and cut the dashed areas out for starting locations. Use three 4" (102mm)-long ¼" (6mm) hex bolts, three wingnuts, two washers, and two outside pointed lockwashers for each bolt. Pattern on page 127.

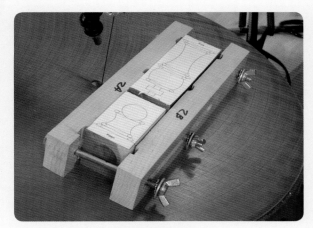

This compound-cutting jig is extremely handy!

8

Begin cutting pieces. Thread the blade into the starting slot and begin cutting. I normally use a #7 blade, in order to be both aggressive and strong enough to take the heat this will generate. Keep in mind that you are cutting lumber that is 1½" (38mm) thick. It will take time to cut through, so be patient.

9

Cut the corners. The 270° cutting technique (page 21) provides sharp corners and reduces the possibility of scorching the piece. In the picture above, the cutting continues past the corner.

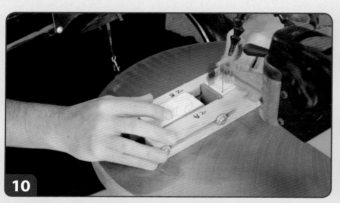

10

Continue cutting corners. Continuing the 270° cut, a circle is cut in the waste part of the pattern, and the cut re-enters at the exact point of the corner.

11

Keep the piece together. Use a clear packing tape to keep the piece together after the first side is cut. Put the two pieces back in the jig, tighten it back up, and check for stability again.

12

Protect the faces. On the second side of the cut, the flat faces on the top of the piece do not need to be cut. The first cut took care of the horizontal cut. Looping above and into the waste part of the pattern, as shown, keeps the corners sharp, and reduces the possibility of messing up the horizontal face.

13

Cut the rest of the pieces. Once all sides are cut, take the piece out of the jig and remove the waste. Be gentle. It would be a shame to break the piece at this point. Repeat the cutting steps for all the pieces. To cut the cheeks of the knight, please see the sidebar (at right).

30

Cutting the Knight

The horsehead knight requires an extra two cuts to narrow the nose and make the piece look more like a horse.

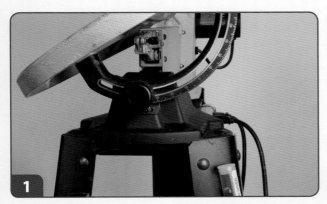

1

Prepare the saw. Tilt the scroll saw table to 30° (left side down).

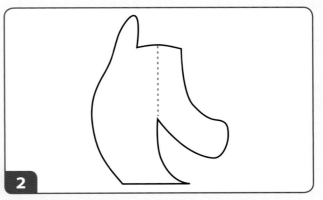

2

Sketch a line. Imagine or draw a line on the piece from the point where the neck intersects the jaw of the horse, vertically to the top of the head. This is the line that will be cut.

3

Make the first cut. Starting from the top of the head, cut the right side of the piece. When you have cut through to the joint, follow the neckline to finish the cut.

4

Make the last cut. Turn the piece over and start with the bottom of the nose and cut through to the top of the head.

5

The end result is a compound-compound cut chess piece.

14

Sand the faces. The base has four faces that need to be sanded. This is easiest by attaching a sheet of sandpaper to a block of wood with adhesive spray and sanding the sides as shown above.

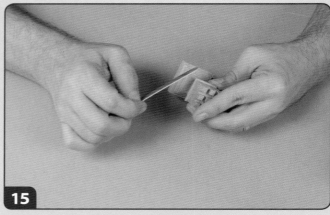

15

Remove fuzzies. Use an emery board to remove the fuzzies from the corners of each piece.

16

Mix epoxy. To put the weights in the bottom, mix a small amount of 30-minute epoxy and use a glue brush to brush the epoxy in a thick coat inside the hole of one of the chess pieces.

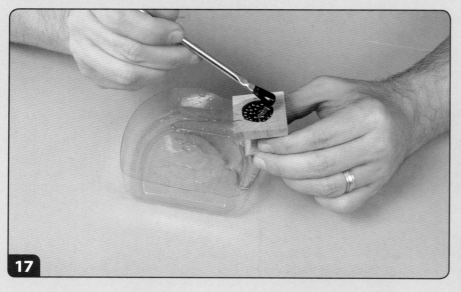

17

Add weights. Fill the base with lead shot, tungsten putty, pennies, or large hex nuts so that none of it sticks above the top of the hole. Use the glue brush to apply the epoxy across the top of the weight and secure all the pieces of the shot.

NOTE: Lead shot is a toxic substance. Be sure to wash your hands after handling the shot.

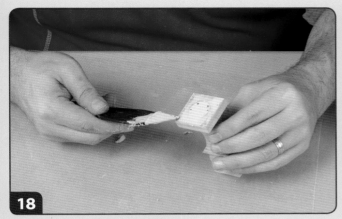

18

Fill the base with wood putty. Let the epoxy fully dry, then fill the hole in the base of the piece with wood putty. It may take more than one application of putty to get the base filled. A light sanding may be necessary. Let the putty dry fully and apply the finish to the piece.

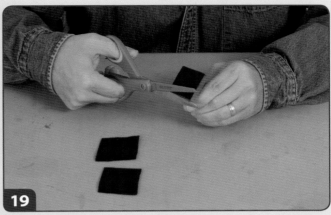

19

Add a felt bottom. The final step is to put a felt bottom on the piece. This can be done with self-stick felt or regular felt attached with spray adhesive.

20

The pieces are complete. Enjoy! The Classic Chess Set is a beautiful pattern that will be treasured for many years to come.

Neo-Classic

With this design, I wanted to push the envelope a little bit and see what would happen if we took a fairly standard design, pushed the waist to one side, and utilized points instead of balls for the top.

The base is very solid and, if used with a heavy or dense lumber, would not need to be weighted for a good feel during play. The twist in the waist will soon have you thinking the pieces are looking particular ways, and if that gives you an advantage when playing, make the most of it.

Please note the points of these pieces can be dangerous if misused. I do not suggest allowing small children to play with them. Also, when storing the pieces, care must be given to those points to preserve them. Storing them in the standing position, or in a box with a nice soft lining, would be recommended.

As you cut these pieces, you may feel like you are doing nothing but circles. The square transition from the base to the waist, the square collars, and multiple points will leave you doing numerous 270° cuts (page 21).

The patterns for this set are on pages 93–95.

Wood Notes

The wood used in this example was hard maple. Maple is a very heavy and hard wood and cuts easily. However, it is very unforgiving if you allow the blade to get hot. Take special care to keep the feed rates low and let the piece and saw determine how fast the cutting will be. Also, on an outside cut, maple will scorch more than half the time. Using the 270° technique will keep sharp edges and also eliminate scorching.

King

The king stands 4" (102mm) tall, and is one of only two pieces with opposing twists. The head of the king is twisted the opposite direction of the waist. The crown of the king is four large spires that point outward toward the corners.

Queen

The queen stands 3⅝" (92mm) tall, and is similar to the king with the opposing twist in the head of the design. The queen's crown is a wide hat with upward-pointed tips. With a veil, you could almost see a demure lady sitting on the throne, being the power behind the king.

Bishop

The bishop stands 3" (76mm) tall and has the same twisted waist as the king and queen. However, the head of the bishop is an upward spire, reminiscent of a church or cathedral spire.

Knight

The knight stands 2¾" (70mm) tall and is based on the same horsehead design as the classic chess set. There was no room to put in a waist with the twist, so the base transitions directly into the head.

Rook

The rook stands 2½" (64mm) tall and has the same waist design as the bishop. The head also utilizes spires in place of the normal castle crenellations.

Pawn

The pawn stands 2¼" (57mm) tall, and has a unique waist among the entire set. The top of the twisted waist is smaller than the base, so it not only twists but reduces until it transitions to the small head that has a single simple spire.

Neo-Classic II

This set is a sequel to the Neo-Classic set. I wanted to take the same twist and use it in a set that had a different feel to it. So where the Neo-Classic set was all about spires and points, this one is more rounded and subtle. The base is unique with a complex ripple to it. I can see cutting this set without the square base and coming from the bottom directly into the ripples.

The patterns for this set are on pages 96–98.

Wood Notes

This set is shown in walnut. As you can see in the picture of the pawn on page 39, there are some variations between the heartwood and sapwood of the lumber. Take time selecting cutting stock for color and grain, and a special set will be the result. Walnut is one of my favorite woods to use for anything. It cuts easily, is rather forgiving in regards to heat, sands easily, and takes a fantastic shine when finished. There is often character hidden in the wood that cannot be seen until the finish is applied. Walnut is often paired with maple, which has similar characteristics, but with a light color and very tight grain.

Cutting Notes

With two minor exceptions, this is a very simple set to cut. If you are looking for a pattern to cut for your first set, this is one that I would recommend. The first exception is the base of each piece, where the bottom slab merges into the complex ripples in a very tight corner. Take your time cutting that and back up and mill that corner out enough to be able to either do the full turn, or take the blade all the way out and back it in before starting to cut the ripples. The second exception is the cross at the top of the king. Be sure to use the 270° cutting technique and cut the detailed side first. When cutting the top on the complimentary side, don't bother to cut the very top flat area—you can just loop around and begin cutting the other side of the cross.

King

The king stands 3⁹⁄₁₆" (91mm) tall. It is characterized by the dual twist that was also seen in the Neo-Classic set. The base is a complex ripple that really is elegant when cut. The collar is moderate and seemingly tight. The headpiece has a large head and small hat area. Overall, it's a simple piece, yet elegant, with the twist being the main design element.

Queen

The queen stands 3⁵⁄₁₆" (84mm) tall, and has the same base, twist, and collar as the king. But the queen features a large, seemingly padded hat that takes design cues from women's hats of the Elizabethan era.

Bishop

The bishop has a single twist to it, again similar to the Neo-Classic set. But instead of an understated collar and emphasized spire, this piece has an exaggerated collar and simple head with no slash. This piece stands 2½" (64mm) tall.

Knight

The knight is the familiar horse head design updated with the Neo Classic II base. Again the design concept was simplicity of form and function. This piece stands 2⁷⁄₁₆" (62mm) tall.

Rook

The rook was a fun piece to design. I was able to back away from the abstract spires theme and use the castle and crenellations. The base and the twist are part of the set design, but the head is the normal castle top, but using curves instead of straight lines. The two outside crenellations lean inward, while the center one is oversize. This piece stands 1¹⁵⁄₁₆" (49mm) tall.

Pawn

The pawn was the easiest of the set to design. I kept the base and twist the same as the rest of the set, transferred a ball from the classic chess set, and squashed it somewhat. The result is a simple easy-to-cut piece with pleasing proportions and curves. This piece measures in at 1⅝" (41mm) tall.

King Henry VIII

England's King Henry VIII was controversial in his time, and remains so. He was responsible for England separating the Church of England from the Catholic Church, and having six wives in a desperate attempt to beget a male heir. This chess set takes many design cues from Henry and his court.

The patterns for this set are on pages 99–101.

King Henry VIII of England inspired this set.

Wood Notes

The examples above are shown in wenge and zebrawood, both of which require a little extra care when used for a chess set. Wenge is a very hard wood, but will cut if special care is taken to keep the heat down. This wood will scorch and actually leave ash in the cut if cutting is rushed. Wenge also splinters easily. Zebrawood is also a scorch-prone wood, but is a little more forgiving than wenge. The effect of the compound cutting on the stripes in zebrawood can create a very striking chess set.

Cutting Notes

The angled entry at the base is actually easier to handle than the perpendicular entry. The collars can be mildly difficult, but not extremely so. All in all, this is a moderately difficult chess set to cut. Use of the milling and 270° cutting techniques (page 21) will be necessary.

King

The entire set takes design cues from the king. The angled entry from the base into the cut is something a bit different, but the key design points are the rotund waist and a high and tight collar. King Henry was known for being obese toward the end of his life, so the entire set features an expanded waist. The king stands 4⅛" (105mm) tall.

Queen

I toyed with the idea of having interchangeable heads on the queen, but that would have been introducing too much complexity to the design. The queen is designed to be demure, yet powerful. She features the same waist and high collar found on the king. She stands 3¾" (95mm) tall.

Bishop

The bishop is also a piece I could have done different things to. Henry separated the Church of England from the Catholic Church, so enhancing or demoting the bishop both could be keeping with the design. However, I again decided to keep it simple, and stayed with the same waist, and introduced a triple rib collar and a relatively small head for the bishop. This piece stands 2⅞" (73mm) tall.

Knight

The knight features a shortened waist with a simple single rib collar before transitioning into the horse head of the knight. This piece stands 2¾" (70mm) tall.

Rook

I did take some license with the rook. I modeled this piece after a dinner goblet, just introducing simple castle crenellations at the top. This piece stands 2⅛" (54mm) tall.

Pawn

The pawn takes the waist from the rook and adds a head that almost seems like the hat a clown might wear. The end result is a squat simple piece that is easily identified as a pawn. This piece stands 2⁵⁄₁₆" (59mm) tall.

Trojan

This design probably had the most re-work of all the designs in the book. The original concept was to make use of four Greek pillars and come up with something unique. For the first few designs, I tried a bent-leg approach, and the pieces ended up looking as if they were rejects from an alien invasion movie. So I shifted my concentration to simple and strong. Keeping with the concepts of strength, poise, and purpose, I set forth to build the Trojan chess set.

The patterns for this set are on pages 102–104.

Wood Notes

In this example, I really bent the rules for compound cutting. The wood shown is mesquite, which is a hard, dense wood that is extremely difficult to cut at any thickness, and very difficult at 1½" (38mm) thick. In cutting this set, I had to revisit about half the pieces, and I actually cut the queen 4 times before I was happy with it. I did learn one trick about mesquite. The fibers of mesquite are long and pliable, which means it's difficult to get a clean cut. So I put the pieces in the cutting jig and put them in the freezer. When the pieces are frozen, the pliability is greatly diminished, providing a clean easy cut. Mesquite will scorch easily, so heat management is something you always have to keep in mind.

Cutting Notes

This design is all sharp edges and straight lines. While the design is simple, cutting this is not something that a beginner should jump into. I suggest this being your third or fourth chess set to get the feel for compound cutting and how to use the jig. Also practice the 270° and the soft landing techniques. When you drill the holes for the inside cuts, make sure you cut perfectly square to the piece. An angled hole will likely go through one of the pillars. The final piece of advice is to cut the inside cuts first. It makes the outside cuts easier and gives you a better grip on the piece.

King

The king is composed of four pillars on top of a square base, standing 4½" (114mm) tall. There is a thin collar and an almost cubic head topped with a cross. It could be argued that in Trojan times, the cross meant something different from what is signified by its use here, but for the purpose of easily identifying the chess king, we will keep it.

Queen

The queen really caused me grief. I had originally designed a head with a hat similar to the Classic queen, but the concept just did not work. Luckily, I found a photograph of a piece of Trojan jewelry that had been recently unearthed in Turkey and used that as the key design for the head. It turned out even better than I imagined once it was cut. The final version stands 3½" (89mm) tall.

Bishop

The bishop embodies simplicity. I used a conical head, squared off to keep with the pillars, and left off the slash in order to simulate the mitre cap of the clergy. The bishop stands a little less than 3⅛" (79mm) tall.

Knight

It would not be a Trojan design if the knight were anything but a horse. I revisited the horsehead design used earlier and made the head a little more svelte. The result is a very noble horse, suited for the Trojan populace to embrace and pull into the city gates. The knight stands just a touch over 3" (76mm) tall.

Rook

Whereas the queen was problematic in design, the rook was simple. A four-corner castle crenellation design on top of the pillars suits this design perfectly. The rook stands 3" (76mm) tall.

Pawn

The pawn's design was also one that went through many changes. My original concept was to mimic a Trojan war helmet, but that will not work with compound cutting. So I then turned a little abstract and utilized a square column, with a smaller square head and a single hole through the head. The hole is meant to signify the visor in a Trojan helmet.

Peter the Great

As I started to design sets based on architecture, I came across a picture of Saint Basil's Cathedral in Red Square in Moscow (see below) and I was hooked. I knew I had to design a chess set around this magnificent building. Peter the Great was instrumental in the spread of chess through Russia. In the year 1700, he struck down a law forbidding the game.

The patterns for this set are on pages 105–107.

St. Basil's Cathedral, in the Red Square in Moscow, was the inspiration behind this chess set.

Wood Notes

For the pieces shown above, I used African mahogany. This is one of the dream woods that can be used for compound cutting. It's a strong, fairly light wood that cuts easily and is very forgiving when it comes to heat tolerance. When finished, the wood has a depth to it that is breathtaking.

Cutting Notes

There are a number of inside cuts and curves with this design. There are also a number of square collars that need to be carefully cut. So for the sharp edges on the collars and the tops of the major pieces, be sure to use the 270° cutting technique. For the rest of the pieces, just take your time and don't force it.

King

The 4½" (114mm) tall king is modeled after one of the domes of the cathedral. The complex curves of the dome are used to shape the head, which also had a large cross at the apex. The tall collar is two square platforms with another complex upswept curve between. The waist of the piece is composed of four pillars with a dual archway design, similar to one of the entranceways of the cathedral.

Queen

The queen also is modeled after the domes of the cathedral, with a small cross swept into the peak. The collar is the same as the king's, and the waist is similar, with a simpler archway. This piece stands 3⅝" (92mm) tall.

Bishop

The bishop was a lot of fun to design. The conical hat is similar to the standard Staunton chess set, but this is the only bishop I've designed that has a head to put the hat on. It is a squat faceless head, but it's there nonetheless. The complex Byzantine archway is modeled after an archway also found on the cathedral. This piece stands 3⅛" (79mm) tall.

Knight

By the time I got to this chess set, I knew that I had to do something different for the knight. When thinking of the different things I could do for the knight, I recalled the simple and elegant look of a saddle on a saddle tree. The design was simple, after the concept, and it turned out very well. Since the Russians have a long history of being remarkable horsemen, the saddle fits the theme. The knight ended up being 2½" (64mm) tall.

Rook

On first glance, the rook for this chess set looks similar to the rook from the Trojan chess set. However, they were designed independently of one another. This castle sports an archway and a second story window, as well as the four-cornered crenellations. This piece stands 2⁷⁄₁₆" (62mm) tall.

Pawn

I knew what I wanted to do for the pawn long before I got down to designing it. The head is modeled after a Russian woman, a scarf holding her hair back, facing forward to defend the motherland.

Canterbury

Wood Notes

The pattern is shown here in walnut and African mahogany. Both of these woods have been discussed in earlier designs.

Cutting Notes

Every piece, with the exception of the knight, features inside cuts. This pattern takes some time to cut. Cutting the king and queen demands patience and care to make sure that the blade is kept straight and not pushed to one side accidentally. Side pressure can cause problems with the inside cuts and the stair-step pattern of the queen. When cutting the outside cut of the pawn, do the side with the peak in the roofline first. Then, when it is turned over, do not cut the level line across the roof. It is already cut, and by cutting it again, you can actually mar the piece.

This small town in the Southeast of the United Kingdom has been influential for centuries. The city holds the seat of the Anglican church, the Canterbury Cathedral, which this set is designed around. This cathedral was the site of the infamous murder of the Archbishop of Canterbury, Thomas Beckett. Beckett, at the time of his murder in 1170, was in a dispute with the king of England, Henry II. Four knights, following Henry's utterance, "Will no one rid me of this turbulent priest?" killed Becket inside the cathedral. Beckett was canonized a few years later, and his tomb in the cathedral attracted many pilgrims; this is documented in Geoffrey Chaucer's fourteenth-century work *Canterbury Tales*.

The patterns for this set are on pages 108–110.

Canterbury Cathedral, located in England, was the inspiration for this set.

King

The king is a representation of the south end of the cathedral itself. The pointed archway windows in the cathedral are all stained glass. The cross at the top was a design addition to make it absolutely clear what piece this was. This is the second tallest piece in this book, standing 5³⁄₁₆" (132mm) tall.

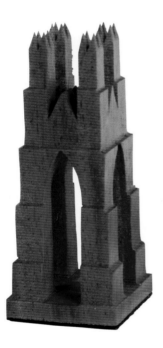

Queen

The queen is a representation of the north end of the cathedral, featuring multiple points on the spires, a soaring doorway, and the stairstep-like progression of the building as it soars heavenward. This piece stands 3¹⁵⁄₁₆" (100mm) high.

Bishop

The head of the bishop is a representation of the headwear for the Archbishop of Canterbury. The large cross cut in the center of the piece accentuates the sanctity of the design. This piece stands 3⅜" (86mm) tall.

Knight

The knight is represented by a saddle. Much of the history of the region deals with not only the cathedral, but also military campaigns, and yes, knights on horseback. This simple little saddle stands 2½" (64mm) tall.

Rook

The design of the rook may look sloppy, but it is a very fair representation of the ruin of the Canterbury Castle, which is separate from the cathedral. Since a ruin is represented, any mistakes made during cutting can be blamed on the pattern, or in keeping with the ruin theme. This little ruin stands 2⁹⁄₁₆" (65mm) high.

Pawn

The pawn is designed after a simple barn or cottage. The everyday people of the bygone era needed a place to sleep, keep livestock, cook meals, raise children, and many other things—all done under the same roof much of the time. This piece is fun to cut, and is very popular with younger players. This piece stands 1¹³⁄₁₆" (46mm) high.

Paris

The word "Paris" itself brings up romantic notions of sidewalk cafés, art, love, and a laid-back lifestyle. I've tried to capture some of that romance in this design. In this design, the king had to be the monument synonymous with Paris, the Eiffel Tower. The queen is the Arc de Triomphe, and the bishop is a fleur-de-lis on a pedestal. The rook is an adaptation of the Bastille, with the inclusion of windows and an arched entryway. The pawns are magnums of champagne. This set began as a test to see if I could build a piece that was faithful to the Eiffel Tower. It took a couple of attempts, but the resultant design is not overly difficult to cut, and is faithful to the proportions of the actual tower. The rest of the designs followed from the Eiffel Tower.

The patterns for this set are on pages 111–113.

Wood Notes

The wood shown in this example is curly maple. I found a slab of 4A curly maple for sale on Ebay. Normally lumber like this is used for a guitar head, or other fine instrument. Luckily for me, this seller was getting out of the instrument business and was selling his blanks. Curly maple has the same characteristics as regular maple, but with a ripple effect once finished. This is striking, unique, and beautiful all at the same time.

Cutting Notes

There are some intricate cuts on the queen and the pawns that work best if you cut one side of them and loop around to cut the other side. The ridges of the queen and the top of the pawn in particular need this additional attention. The rook has some very narrow windows, and if you use a ⅛" (3mm) drill bit, you don't have much wiggle room. Make sure you are absolutely perpendicular to the piece when you drill the starting holes. The bishop has some intricate acute angle cuts that take a little extra care as well. This is not a difficult design to cut, but it does take a little extra time and attention to get everything out of it.

King

The king, as the Eiffel Tower, standing 3¹³⁄₁₆" (99mm) tall, is a very iconic piece. It is instantly recognizable, and you will get comments from everyone who sees it. The design uses the same proportions as the tower itself, and has the same graceful curves and solid decks. While it would have been impossible to put the antenna at the top of the tower, the observation deck at the very top is well represented in this design.

Queen

The queen, as the Arc de Triomphe, is another monument synonymous with Paris. This design stands 2¼" (57mm) tall, and the pattern is altered a bit from the actual proportions to make it taller. The monument, built by Napoleon, was to be a centerpiece in his triumphant return to Paris. However, a British general and a little battle called Waterloo got in the way.

Bishop

The fleur-de-lis is a symbol that resonates with many people as French. Tradition says that it is associated with the Holy Trinity, corresponding to the three petals in the design. Its associations with France and the Church made it a natural as the bishop for this design. The fleur-de-lis sits on a pedestal sloping up off of the base, with a diamond-edged top, transitioning into the flower itself. The piece stands 2⅝" (67mm) tall.

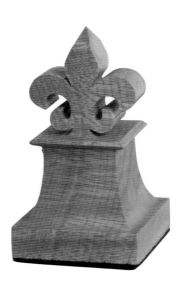

Knight

The knight takes the form of a noble horsehead on a concave pedestal. The head is altered from the original horsehead found in the Classic chess set. This piece stands $2^{13}/_{16}$" (71mm) tall.

Rook

The rook is a representation of the infamous Bastille citadel. This fortress/prison was a touchpoint for the French Revolution. It was demolished in 1789. The version in the design takes the heavy fortress and gives it four towers with small crenellations, and a large arched entryway. This piece, standing $2^{3}/_{16}$" (56mm) tall, is truly iconic in its representation of the classic concepts of chess pieces.

Pawn

I had some fun with designing the pawn. I tried out a coffee cup, a peasant scarf; nothing worked. So keeping with the French theme, I thought that not much is more French than a magnum of champagne (the drink is named after the region in France where the grapes are grown). So I modeled the pawn after a magnum, which is a 1.5 liter bottle—probably the largest that is commonly distributed. This piece is $2^{3}/_{16}$" (56mm) tall.

Roman Glory

Wood Notes

The examples here are done in padauk and Spanish cedar. Both are excellent woods for compound cutting. Padauk will be a bright orange color when first cut, but will turn a deep red when the finish is applied, and may darken further as it ages. It is only moderately tolerant of heat, so care must be taken on corners. Personally, I enjoy padauk for a simple reason—the smell of the wood reminds me of the smell of my grandmother's kitchen when she baked cookies.

Spanish cedar is also a very accommodating and forgiving wood for compound cutting. When cutting this, I do recommend using a mask because there is an oil in the wood that can cause reactions in some people. Sadly, this wood does not smell like fresh-baked cookies, but medicinal alcohol.

I knew at the start of the design of this set that it was going to be something special. Many of the pieces were inspired by digital recreations of the Roman Forum. This set also has two bases for the pieces. The king, queen, and pawn use a simple column platform base, while the rook, knight, and bishop have a more intricate multiple-column base.

The patterns for this set are on pages 114–116.

Cutting Notes

This is an advanced design that should not be undertaken unless you are comfortable and experienced with compound cutting. There are a number of inside cuts that are challenging, and the inside cuts of the king can almost seem monotonous. But if care is taken, this design can make a very special set that will be cherished for many years to come.

King

The king is a large, intricate piece modeled after the Colosseum. I tried to capture the southwest entryway of the Colosseum, with the different setback levels and the multiple arches. On the side with the slope, the Colosseum today is missing much of the artwork and adornment that was there when it was built. So I designed in some rather ragged edges, trying to give the piece a little flavor of time. This piece stands 4⅛" (105mm) tall.

Queen

The queen is modeled after the Roman columns within the Roman Forum. The top of the column is adorned with a simple leaf design, and because of the size of the piece, it is difficult to get very detailed. This majestic piece stands 3¹¹⁄₁₆" (94mm) tall.

Bishop

The bishop is modeled after a reconstruction of the Temple of Vesta. Vesta was the Roman goddess of the home, hearth, and family. This temple was where the Vestal Virgins, the only female priests in the Roman theological system, tended the eternal flame. Inside the main opening of the piece is a hearth that the Priestesses would ensure burned continuously. The multi-column base transitions directly into the temple itself. This piece stands 3³⁄₁₆" (81mm) tall.

Knight

The knight was a challenge. I could re-use the horse head again, or come up with something different. On a fluke, I found a picture of an actual Roman saddle, and it featured the distinctive four horns. At first it confused me, but then I remembered that the stirrup was not invented until the middle ages—the four horns are for the horseman to hang on to. This piece stands 2¾" (70mm) tall.

Rook

The rook is designed after a roman fortress in France, called the Citadel of Carcassonne. This design is a tall flat-sided tower with very narrow slits between the crenellations. This piece stands 2¾" (70mm) tall.

Pawn

The pawn is a simple Roman column. The column is rather short with a large base. The proportions of this piece are similar to the proportions found in a simulation of what the Roman Forum could have looked like. This piece stands 2⅜" (60mm) tall.

San Francisco

I had originally envisioned this set being used as a way to illustrate design methods, but as I got deeper into the design, I found out I had a very intricate design here, and using it as an instructional tool would not be the best idea. So I shelved that idea and stuck with the set. San Francisco is one of the iconic cities in the USA. Many of the icons and sights of San Francisco are found here in this set.

The patterns for this set are on pages 117–119.

Wood Notes

The wood used for the examples above is sapele. This African wood cuts and behaves much like African mahogany, but with a finer, deeper grain. It also has ripple and other detail in the wood that most likely will not be seen until the finish is applied. Sapele is very forgiving and very tolerant of heat. It's a heavy and dense wood, so is well-suited to a chess set that does not have weights.

Cutting Notes

This is one of the most intricate sets to cut. The most intricate piece is the pawn. Make sure to take care and go slow when cutting. Going too fast will ruin the pieces. In this set, I introduce a new type of base. This base is cut from the bottom, not from the side. It provides the piece a furniture-type of base to rest upon. When cutting the base, cut the arch first; then enter the pattern from the bottom. Once you get used to starting at the bottom, it's no problem.

King

The king is modeled after one of the towers of the Golden Gate Bridge. I would have liked to cut the entire bridge, but that would not work for a chess piece. This tower, or pier, is faithful to the original proportions. When finished it will stand 4½" (114mm) tall.

Queen

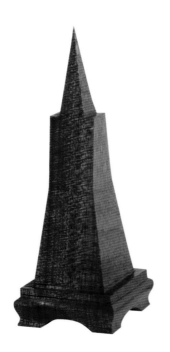

The queen is modeled after the TransAmerica Pyramid. The proportions on this piece are a little short compared to the actual tower, but it makes a more stable and sturdy piece and allows the king to be taller. This piece stands 4" (102mm) tall.

Bishop

The bishop is inspired by the Cathedral of Saint Mary. The complex curves and proportions of the building could not be duplicated in a compound-cut chess piece, so I took some of the curves and used them. The cross in the center is representative of Saint Mary's and its Catholic heritage. This piece is 2¾" (70mm) tall.

Knight

The knight is another horse head design. I used the updated version that has a better nose-on profile. I really wanted to make something commemorating the fire horses that pulled the steam driven engines during efforts to fight the great fire in 1906. However, images of that time are few and far between—so I compromised and put the normal horse head on the furniture base. This piece is 2⁵⁄₁₆" (59mm) tall.

Rook

The rook is modeled after the Coit Tower, commemorating the firefighters from the 1906 earthquake and fire. Though the actual tower is cylindrical, that would have been difficult to do with a compound cut, so I transferred the feel of the tower to a rectangular piece. I broke with tradition and made this tower taller than all the other pieces, with the exception of the king and queen. The windows at the top of the piece are small and a sure hand must be used when drilling the holes for the inside cuts. When complete, this piece is 3⅝" (92mm) tall.

Pawn

The pawn is the beloved cable car. One side represents the front and back of the car, complete with a hole where the headlight would be, and the other side has the doorways on and off the car. The pawns are tough to cut, but very rewarding. They look amazing lined up on a chessboard ready to do battle. This piece is 2¼" (57mm) tall.

Venice

Wood Notes

Goncalo alves (also known as tigerwood or marblewood) was used in the examples above. This wood is a bit difficult to work with, especially when cutting thicknesses more than ½" (13mm). Therefore, cutting wood 1½" (38mm) thick is problematic. Goncalo alves is also not very forgiving with heat and will scorch. So the best advice is just to go slow. Let your saw blade pull the piece instead of pushing the piece into the blade. This wood also really comes to life when finished. The dark stripes get darker when finished and the contrast and patterns are truly magnificent.

Cutting Notes

This is a very intricate set to cut, and it will take a lot of time and patience. This pattern also uses a base that is cut from the bottom and is much like the hull of a ship. Be sure to use the 270° technique (page 21) to get good sharp corners on the base and many other places in the set.

Venice is a very interesting place, so I made a very interesting set to go along with it. Venice was a city-state in the northwest part of what would become Italy. It was not conquered until taken over by Napoleon in 1797, which ended 1,070 years of independence. Venice is noted for its naval and military strength, as well as being a trade center for hundreds of years. Four of the pieces are modeled after buildings found on St. Mark's Square, a central landmark of this canal-crossed city.

The patterns for this set are on pages 120–122.

St. Mark's Square in Venice inspired many of the pieces in this set. The bell tower (back center) influenced the design of the king; the Lion of Venice (front center), the queen; and the Doge's Palace (right), the rook.

King

The king is modeled after the bell tower in St. Mark's Square. This 323-foot (99 meter) tower was completed in 1514 and stood until 1902, when it collapsed. It was rebuilt again in 1912. This piece mimics the eight windows on the shaft of the tower, which are too small to be cut, by using a ¹⁄₁₆" (2mm) drill bit to drill partway into the piece. I would not recommend drilling all the way through. The arches at the top are of close proportion to the actual tower, and the high peak roof is as well. This is the largest chess piece I have ever designed, standing at 5¹³⁄₁₆" (148mm) tall. It is very impressive on a board or shelf.

Queen

The queen is patterned after the Lion of Venice that stands on a column in St. Mark's Square. There is a pair of columns in the Piazza San Marco: one for each of Venice's patrons. The lion is symbolic of St. Mark. The actual lion has wings and a long flowing tail. Due to size constraints, the wings had to be consolidated, and the tail left off, but it's still impressive. This piece stands 4" (102mm) tall.

Bishop

The bishop is patterned after St. Mark's Basilica itself. This cathedral, which was built in the year 832 and added to over the next 800 years, is one of the best examples of Byzantine architecture in existence today. That Byzantine influence can be seen in this piece: flowing spires, a hint of influence from an Arabian minaret, and windows that flow up to a point. The dome itself also has a flowing point. This piece stands 3" (76mm) tall.

Knight

The knight, once again, was a most troublesome piece. Venice is not known for their cavalry or mounted knights. Venice was a seafaring community with a very strong military that utilized each person's two feet. In doing research, I found the solution in a present-day saddle. This piece is modeled after a Venetian dressage saddle. Dressage is a form of horsemanship in which the rider guides the horse with touches of the knees and toes so no outward motion or guidance is seen. This piece stands 2⁵⁄₁₆" (59mm) tall.

Rook

The rook is modeled after the Doge's Palace, also on St. Mark's Square. This gothic palace, which housed the Doge and the offices of the Republic of Venice, was completed in its current form in 1442. The palace's façade has row upon row of pointed windows with round windows interspersed. The windows—large, small, and round—are all faithful to the actual palace. The pointed crenellations at the top are ornamental, and were not used to provide archers or crossbowmen places to hide behind between shots. This piece is 2¾" (70mm) tall.

Pawn

The pawn is a representation of the Rialto Bridge in Venice. Completed in 1581, this covered bridge, which crosses the Canal Grande, is made of stone. Stone was used because the two previous bridges either were burned or collapsed under the weight of the foot traffic and crowds. The piece represents the center section of the bridge, with an archway that allows the canal and boats to pass underneath. This piece is 1¾" (44mm) tall.

The travel chess set.

3 Projects

This section presents you with four projects to build: a chessboard, a storage box, a travel chess set, and a vertical chess set. Some of the projects are long and involved, and some are simple. Take your time and have fun building them. I assure you, I had a blast putting them together.

Making a Chessboard

If you have fantastic chess pieces, you need a good chessboard. Luckily, chessboards are actually easy to build, and spectacular when complete. The board can be built to match a chess set, or built to match a décor. Just pick two contrasting woods and get started! I constructed the step-by-step board from paduak, canarywood, and cherry.

Materials and Tools

Tools
- Table saw
- Belt sander
- Random orbit sander
- Clamps
- Router
- Router table
- ½" (13mm)-radius roundover router bit
- Gluing jig (see inset)

Materials
- (3) 18½" x 2" x 1" (470mm x 51mm x 25mm) dark wood strips
- (1) 18½" x 2½" x 1" (470mm x 64mm x 25mm) dark wood strip
- (3) 18½" x 2" x 1" (470mm x 51mm x 25mm) light wood strips
- (1) 18½" x 2½" x 1" (470mm x 64mm x 25mm) light wood strip
- (14) 2" x 2½" x 1" (51mm x 64mm x 25mm) border pieces
- (2) 20" x 2½" x 1" (508mm x 64mm x 25mm) border strips
- Waxed paper
- Wood glue
- Spray adhesive
- Felt
- Danish oil

Making a Chessboard

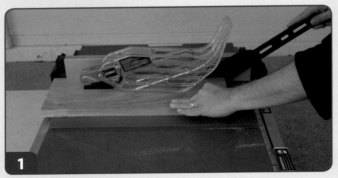

Cut the wood. To create 2" (51mm) squares, you need four strips of light-colored wood and four strips of dark-colored. One light and one dark strip are 2½" (64mm) wide and 18½" (470mm) long. Three light and three dark strips are 2" (51mm) wide and 18½" (470mm) long. The extra length makes room for the kerf later.

Square Clamping Jig

The jig is built from a 2' x 4' (.6m x 1.2m) section of ¾" (19mm) medium-density fiberboard (MDF). The jig is a 20" (508mm) square piece of MDF, with 2" x 15" (51mm x 381mm) strips that are glued and nailed exactly square.

Square clamping jig.

Glue alternating strips together. Put down waxed paper on the jig. Put the wider strips on the outsides; the extra width will accommodate a ½" (13mm) lap joint for the border. Apply glue on the strip sides and line them up. The jig will keep all sides square, tight, and flat. Put more waxed paper on top.

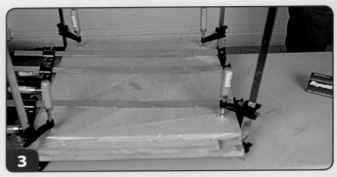

Clamp the jig. With the two pieces of the jig put together, clamp the jig to compress the glue joints and keep the two halves of the jig tightly closed. Keep the board in the jig for 4 to 6 hours so the glue can set.

Cut the strips. Remove the board from the jig. Allow it to dry overnight. Cut the board into six 2" (51mm)-wide strips and two 2½" (64mm)-wide strips crosswise to the direction of the colored strips.

Glue up the squares. Put the freshly cut strips in the jig again. This time, glue the strips so the light and dark squares alternate. Place the wider strips on the outside. Order the strips carefully to ensure good fit and the best-looking board possible. Glue, clamp in the jig, and allow drying time as in steps 2 and 3.

Cut the border strips. To keep the direction of the grain consistent, the border is composed of two long border strips and two strips glued together from eight pieces. Use a board clamped in a miter saw to cut the small 2" (51mm) wide strips for the glued-up strips.

Glue the composite strips. Glue the short strips together so the grain runs parallel to the glue joint. Use the jig to keep the pieces tight and square.

Cut the lap joints. Cut a ½" (13mm)-wide lap joint on the end grain sides of the board with the contrasting squares. Also cut lap joints on the glued-up border strips.

Attach the glued-up border to the board. Glue the glued-up border pieces to the lapped ends of the board, keeping the glue joints lined up. Clamp and allow to dry overnight.

Cut the remaining lap joints. Cut the remaining lap joints on the board and the last two side strips. Glue them together. I made the strips longer than the board so I could trim the excess after the glue had dried.

Belt-sand the surface. Even with the jig and careful gluing, there will likely be some differences in the height of the squares. Use a belt sander with a 60-grit belt to even out the surface. Use a 120-grit belt to sand a bit finer.

12

Finish-sand the surface. Use the random orbit sander with 120-grit sandpaper to remove the last of the tool marks. Then use 220-grit sandpaper to make the surface even smoother.

13

Rout the edges. Set up the router and router table to be able to dress up the edge of the board. Above, I used a ½" (13mm)-radius roundover bit.

14

Fill in any gaps. Use one part sawdust, one part wood glue, and one part water. Go back over the playing surface and fill in any gaps with the appropriate sawdust mixture. Allow this wood putty to dry, and then sand the board with the random orbit sander and 220-grit sandpaper.

15

Apply Danish oil. Apply a thick coat of Danish oil to the top and bottom of the board. The board needs to be finished on both sides so moisture doesn't cause it to crack. Let the board sit for 30 minutes. Apply a light coat and then wipe dry. Allow the oil to cure overnight.

Wood Movement

Changes in relative humidity cause wood to shrink and expand across the grain, but not along the grain. The movement in length is negligible. But the movement in width and thickness is inevitable, and in some woods it can be ³⁄₁₆" to ¼" (5mm to 6mm) per foot of width under typical weather conditions—*after* the wood has been air or kiln dried. The density of the wood, the way it is finished, and the species all determine how the wood will change size. The chessboard is a problematic project with small pieces of different wood species glued together.

Ways to counteract movement include keeping the direction of the grain consistent throughout the board as we have done, or using thin tiles or veneer glued to plywood backing.

16

Apply felt backing. The final step is to use the spray adhesive to apply a felt backing to the board. Once the felt is tightly applied, use scissors or a very sharp knife to remove the excess felt.

Simple Storage Box

One thing I didn't understand about chess sets until I started to build them is you need a place to store them. Keeping them on a board, set up nice and neat, won't work in a normal household. The kids, the cats, and normal everyday life are hazards to the health of your chess set. One solution would be to use a plastic craft or tackle box, but that is almost sacrilegious when so much work has been put into the chessmen. So, the easiest wood solution is to use a craft box found at your local craft or hobby store.

The patterns for this project are on page 123.

Materials and Tools

Tools
❖ Scroll saw
❖ Screwdriver

Materials
❖ 12.25" x 9.8" x 3.2" (311mm x 249mm x 81mm) unfinished decoupage memory box from craft store
❖ 2' x 2' x ¼" (610mm x 610mm x 6mm) MDF
❖ Cyanoacrylate glue
❖ Cyanoacrylate activator
❖ Blue painter's tape
❖ Spray adhesive
❖ 12" x 12" x ⅛" (305mm x 305mm x 3mm) Baltic birch plywood

1

Apply painter's tape to the MDF. The majority of the work for this box is done with the tray and dividers. The box is pre-made, and the lid works great, so the first step is to apply blue painter's tape to the MDF in preparation for cutting out the dividers.

2

Attach the divider patterns. Use the spray adhesive to attach the pattern for the dividers to the MDF.

3

Cut out the dividers. Use the scroll saw to cut the dividers according to the pattern. The pattern shows how many pieces are needed for each level. There are two levels to the storage box. It may be simpler to use a stack-cutting process to cut the multiple copies of the dividers.

4

Assemble the dividers. Assemble the dividers according to the illustration at right. Use the CA glue and activator to glue the dividers to the bottom of the box.

5

Cut the birch plywood to size. Cut the birch plywood to 8⅝" x 11⅛" (219mm x 283mm). This is ⅛" (3mm) less than the inner dimensions of the box.

6

Assemble the second layer of dividers. Assemble the dividers on the birch, using CA glue and activator.

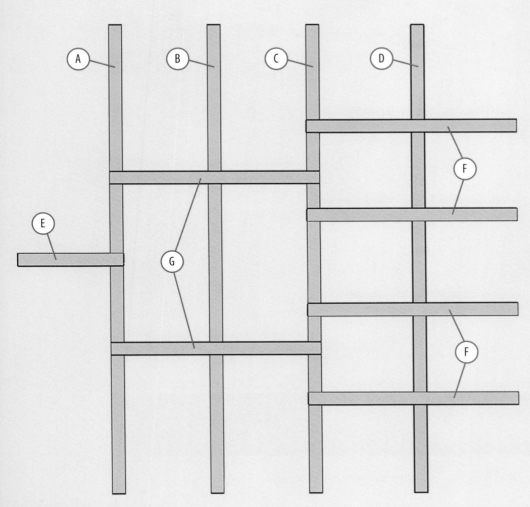

Divider assembly diagram.

7

Check that the layer fits in the box. When complete, the storage box has space to store the 32 pieces of a full chess set. This box will store any of the sets in this book, with the exception of the Venice chess set.

8

Insert pieces. The dividers will rise above the top of the box, but that is normal. Now you have proper storage for your new chess set!

Travel Chess Set

This project was given to me as a challenge, and it certainly was a challenge

to design and build. Downsizing the pieces to a 1" x 1" (25mm x 25mm)

compound pattern meant that they needed to be simpler in design. The

pieces are patterned after the long-lived Staunton design. The case contains

both the board and the storage for the pieces. The pieces and the board have

magnets embedded so you can play chess in a moving car, in a heavy wind,

or travelling just about anywhere.

The patterns for this project are on pages 124–126.

Making the Travel Chess Set

Materials and Tools

Tools

- Table saw
- Scroll saw
- Clamps
- Router
- Router table
- ¼" roundover router bit
- Flush-cut router bit
- Variable speed drill
- ⁵⁄₆₄" (1.9mm) brad point drill bit
- ¼" (6mm) brad point drill bit
- Utility knife
- Paintbrush
- Mini-flocking tool
- Random orbit sander
- Putty knife
- Measuring tape
- Drill press
- ⁷⁄₁₆" (11mm) Forstner drill bit
- 1" (25mm) scroll saw jig (see page 78)
- Scissors
- Combination square
- Screwdriver
- Needlenose pliers
- Plastic putty knife
- (2) 1" paintbrushes

Materials

- (8) 1⅜" x 12" x ½" (35mm x 305mm x 13mm) light wood strips
- (8) 1⅜" x 12" x ½" (35mm x 305mm x 13mm) dark wood strips
- (2) 2½" x 11" x ½" (64mm x 279mm x 13mm) dark border strips
- (2) 2½" x 16" x ½" (64mm x 406mm x 13mm) dark border strips
- (2) 2½" x 11" x ½" (64mm x 279mm x 13mm) light border strips
- (2) 2-½" x 16" x ½" (64mm x 406mm x 13mm) light border strips
- (3) 4" x 14" x ½" (102mm x 356mm x 13mm) dark planks
- (1) 4" x 14" x ½" (102mm x 356mm x 13mm) light plank
- (14) 14" x ¾" x ½" (356mm x 19mm x 13mm) sticks for dividers
- (1) Plastic case handle
- (2) 1⁵⁄₁₆" x 2⅛" (33mm x 54mm) brass-plated draw latches
- (2) 36mm x 34mm brass-plated lid dowels
- (22) #4 x ½" (13mm) brass screws
- (36) Black head upholstery tacks
- (4) 14" x 1" (356mm x 25mm) elastic strips
- Wood glue
- Blue painter's tape
- Spray adhesive
- Colored flock adhesive
- Colored flocking
- Danish oil
- Wood putty
- (64) ¼" x ¼" (6mm x 6mm) cylinder rare earth magnets
- (32) 0.4" x 0.05" (10mm x 1.3mm) disk rare earth magnets
- Cyanoacrylate glue
- Cyanoacrylate activator

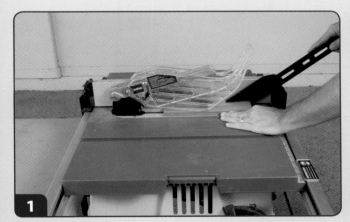

1

Cut the stock. The first step is to cut the individual wood pieces.

2

Glue two chessboards together. Assemble two chessboards using the 1⅜" (35mm)-wide pieces of wood. Follow the instructions in the chessboard section for details (page 65). The border of one of the boards will be dark wood, and the other will be made of light wood. When the boards are assembled, glue the 11" (279mm) border pieces to opposite sides of both the light and dark sides. When that is dry, glue the 16" (406mm) pieces to the two remaining sides for each board. These glued-up boards are now the basis for the top and bottom of the case.

3

Transfer pattern to boards. Sand the boards and prepare them for the scroll saw. When they are ready, transfer the pattern to the boards, using the center of the chessboard as the center for the pattern. Use the measurements from the pattern and carefully measure and draw the pattern directly to the wood.

4

Transfer pattern to sides of box. Apply the patterns to the sides of the box, either by using a printed pattern or by transferring the pattern using measurements.

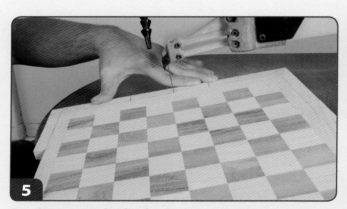

5

Cut the tops and sides for the box using the scroll saw.

6

Fit the box together. Carefully fit the top, bottom, and sides together and trim as necessary, using a utility knife or sharp chisel. Mark the sides, top, and bottom to ensure the fitted pieces are glued together in the same position.

7

Glue the box together, using liberal coats of wood glue.

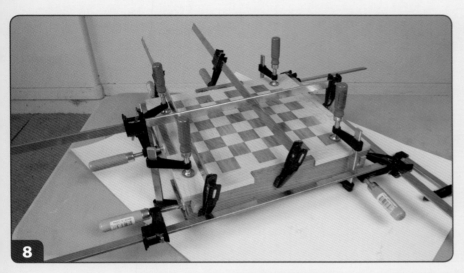

8 Clamp the box together and let it dry overnight.

9

Trim the faces. Use a flush cut router bit on a router table to trim the excess from the long fingers on each face. When that is complete, use a ¼" (6mm) roundover bit to dress up all of the edges.

10

Cut the box open. *NOTE: The only way to complete the next step is to remove the safety guard from the table saw. Please use extra caution.* Set up the table saw to cut 1" (25mm) from the top of the box, and set the depth just short of the thickness of the wood. Cut all four sides, taking care to keep the same face against the saw fence for all four cuts.

11

Finish cutting open the box. Use a utility knife to finish separating the top of the box from the bottom. Clean up the cut with the utility knife or a sharp chisel.

12

Fill the gaps and sand. Fill the gaps in the top and the bottom of the box with wood putty. When the putty is dry, sand the top and bottom to 220 grit.

Apply Danish oil. Use Danish oil to finish the outside and inner lip of the top and bottom of the box.

Mark the squares' centers. On the inside of the top of the box, use a straight edge to mark the center of each of the 64 squares of the chessboard.

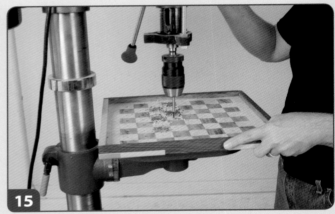

Drill holes for magnets. Use a ¼" (6mm) brad point drill bit in a drill press to drill a hole in the center of each square from the inside of the top of the box. The depth of the hole should be just a paper thickness more than ¼" (6mm) deep.

Check the magnets. Verify the polarity of the magnets before gluing them into the top of the box. If you opted to make the chess pieces first, you can use those to check the polarity. The side that is attracted to the chess piece should go into the hole.

17

Glue the magnets. Use CA glue to attach the ¼" x ¼" (6mm x 6mm) cylinder magnets to the inside of the box top.

18

Apply putty. When the CA glue is dry, use a plastic putty knife to apply wood putty to fill in any depressions left by the magnets. Allow the wood putty to dry and sand with a sanding block.

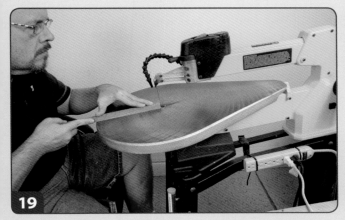

19

Cut the dividers. Cut the dividers as per the pattern shown on page 125. If necessary, you can use smaller pieces of scrap wood. Just make sure the separation will be under another cross divider.

20

Assemble dividers. Assemble the dividers in the bottom of the box and glue them to the bottom using CA glue.

21

Apply flocking. Flock both the inside of the top and bottom of the box. Do one side first, then the other. The working time for the flocking adhesive is very short. Use a 1" (25mm) cheap paintbrush to apply the adhesive, as shown above, then use the mini-flocker to apply the flock. Allow the flocking to dry for 24 hours before shaking the excess flock off.

22

Apply elastic. Use the upholstery tacks to attach the elastic strips over the places for the pieces. Two tacks per cross divider works best.

23

Install latches. Select the side for the handle. The sides to the left and right of the handle side will have the lid dowels and draw latches installed. Both the lid dowels and the draw latches are located 2½" (64mm) from the front and back of the box. Line up the latch and dowel and mark the holes. Drill them with the 5⁄64" (1.9mm) drill bit, taking care to not drill all the way through the wood, and attach the hardware with the #4 brass wood screws. Put the latches on opposite corners, to keep the lid securely attached. For the lid dowels, attach the male piece to the bottom of the box.

24

Install handle. Locate the centerline on the front of the box and center the handle on the line. Mark the holes for the screws and drill them with the 5⁄64" (1.9mm) drill bit, taking care to not drill all the way through the side. Attach the handle with the #4 wood screws.

1" (25mm) Scroll Saw Jig

The 1" (25mm) scroll saw compound cutting jig is a simpler version of the larger jig. Cut the two pieces according to the pattern and drill the holes for the bolts. Use 3" (76mm) hex bolts and wing nuts to fasten the jig together.

Making the Pieces

The pieces are very similar to the rest of the designs in this book, with one main difference: they are based off of 1" x 1" (25mm x 25mm) stock. I've created a very simple jig for use with the 1" (25mm) chess pieces. Please see sidebar at left for details.

Prepare the stock. Prepare the stock as you would with any chess piece, cutting sticks of 1" by 1" lumber, applying the blue painter's tape and the pattern with spray adhesive. Use a ⁷⁄₁₆" (11mm) Forstner drill bit in a drill press to drill a ⅛" (3mm)-deep hole. These holes will house the magnets.

Cut the pieces. Cut the pieces using the jig. Cut one side, apply clear packing tape to hold the piece together, and then cut the other side.

Install magnets. To apply the magnets, put a liberal amount of CA glue in the hole under each piece.

Check the polarity. Take care to keep the polarity of the magnets the same for all pieces. If the box is complete, check the polarity using the board on top of the box. Place the magnet with the correct polarity facing up, and press the magnet into the CA glue with a pencil or piece of wooden scrap. Use CA activator to freeze the magnet in place.

Apply wood putty. Using a plastic putty knife, fill the hole on the bottom of the piece with wood putty. Sand it flat after the putty dries. Finish the piece with spray finish, such as polyurethane. Add the felt bottom to the piece and cut the felt to fit with a sharp pair of scissors.

Vertical Chess Set

Just when you thought you had seen all the ideas that could come along for the game of chess, somebody goes and designs a chess set that hangs on a wall. To be honest, it's a radical idea, but one that really opens up design possibilities. So I've taken a stab at this type of set, and this is what I've come up with.

The design concept behind the board and set was the country of Germany. When I think of European cities and walls, the first thing that comes to mind is the Berlin wall. I would have loved to use Berlin as the main design point, but that design had some limitations, so I broadened my scope to all of Germany. The main coat of arms is Germany's. I've taken a few liberties with the eagle in order to put more of a body to it, but the main essence is there. The upright bear is the coat of arms for Berlin, and the key is the coat of arms for Bremen. The fretwork flourish at the top and bottom corners follow a general floral design that ties the three coats of arms into the board as a whole.

The board has 4" x 2" (102mm x 51mm) squares. When the chessboard is translated into a vertical position, the proportions are thrown off-kilter a little, so I added two storage columns on each side of the board. A strip of contrasting wood separates the board from the storage. Another concern I had was knocking the pieces everywhere, so I put magnets in the shelves and the pieces.

The design uses three contrasting colors of wood and a ½" (13mm) Baltic birch backing. The woods used in this example are maple, walnut, and padauk. The pieces that go with the board are made of walnut and spalted curly maple. The result is a striking project that is built to last for years and be beautiful at the same time.

Building this project, which consists of more than 350 individual pieces, is challenging. The construction consists of four major construction steps:

1. The board tiles and the backing

2. The shelves and frame

3. The flourishes and coats of arms

4. The chess pieces

The patterns for this project are

on pages 128–134.

Materials and Tools

Tools
- Scroll saw
- Table saw
- Router
- Router table
- ¼" (6mm) roundover router bit
- ¼" (6mm) Roman ogee router bit
- Brad nailer
- Screwdriver
- Clamps

Materials
- (1) 25" x 31½" x ½" (635mm x 800mm x 13mm) Baltic birch backing board
- (1) 26" x 2¾" x ½" (660mm x 70mm x 13mm) dark wood for top frame
- (2) 39" x 2¾" x ½" (991mm x 70mm x 13mm) dark wood for frame sides
- (1) 26" x 2¾" x ¼" (660mm x 70mm x 6mm) dark wood for outer half of bottom frame
- (1) 26" x 2" x ¼" (660mm x 51mm x 6mm) dark wood for inner half of bottom frame
- (14) 26" x 2" x ¼" (660mm x 51mm x 6mm) dark wood for shelf halves
- (2) ½" x 31½" x ¼" (13mm x 800mm x 6mm) dark wood for playing surface divider
- (2) 5" x 5" x ¼" (127mm x 127mm x 6mm) dark wood for two small coats of arms
- (1) 9" x 9" x ¼" (229mm x 229mm x 6mm) medium wood for large coat of arms
- (2) 5" x 5" x ¼" (127mm x 127mm x 6mm) light wood platforms for small coats of arms
- (1) 9" x 9" x ¼" (229mm x 229mm x 6mm) light wood for large coat of arms
- (32) 2" x 4" x ¼" (51mm x 102mm x 6mm) light wood tiles for playing surface
- (32) 2" x 4" x ¼" (51mm x 102mm x 6mm) medium wood tiles for playing surface
- (4) 4" x 4" x ¼" (102mm x 102mm x 6mm) medium wood for corners and crown fretpiece
- (16) 4" x 4" x ¼" (102mm x 102mm x 6mm) light wood for storage backing, corners and crown fretpieces
- (24) 2" x 2" x ¼" (51mm x 51mm x 6mm) shelf braces as per pattern
- (16) 2" x 2" x ¾" (51mm x 51mm x 19mm) shelf braces (glued stock, see instructions)
- (96) 0.4" x 0.05" (10mm x 1.3mm) disk rare earth magnets
- (32) ¼" x ¼" (6mm x 6mm) cylinder rare earth magnets
- (1) 36" x 17" x ¼" (914mm x 432mm x 6mm) light wood board (glued up) for crown flourish
- (2) 8" x 8" x ¼" (203mm x 203mm x 6mm) light wood boards for lower left and lower right flourish
- (2) ¼" x 4" x 10" (6mm x 102mm x 254mm) wood boards for backing supports
- 26" x 2½" x 1" (660mm x 64mm x 25mm) dark wood for crenellations
- Blue painter's tape
- Polyurethane spray finish
- Waterproof wood glue
- Wood glue
- Cyanoacrylate glue
- Cyanoacrylate activator
- 1" (25mm) brads
- 55" x 1½" x 1½" (1397mm x 38mm x 38mm) chess piece stock (dark)
- 55" x 1½" x 1½" (1397mm x 38mm x 38mm) chess piece stock (light)
- Felt
- (2) 50 pound picture hanging kits
- (16) #4 x ¾" (19mm) wood screws

Making the Vertical Chess Set

Part 1: Board tiles and backing

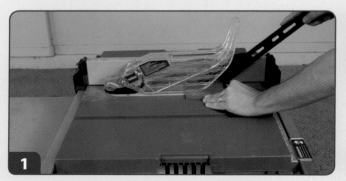

Prepare the materials. Cut the tiles, separator, storage tiles, corners, and blanks for the crowns as per the materials list.

Cut out the crowns according to the patterns.

Cut out the backing board. Cut the backing board according to the materials list. Find the center of the board and use two straight edges clamped to the board as guides to glue the tiles to the backing. Make sure one corner of one of the four quadrants is actually the center; be sure to start here when laying tiles. I used two steel yardsticks clamped to the backing board.

Attach the first quarter of the tiles. Work from the center of the board and use waterproof wood glue to attach individual tiles onto the backing board by quadrant. Test-fit every tile, and if there are fuzzies or splinters left from cutting the tiles, use sandpaper to remove them before gluing.

Avoiding wood movement issues

My major concern with this board is the possibility of changes in the wood due to pressure, temperature, and humidity loosening and popping off the tiles. Waterproof wood glue minimizes the effect of these environmental forces, and has a little more elasticity than normal wood glue.

Attach the rest of the tiles. When the first quadrant of the playing surface is complete, remove one of the straight edges and complete another quadrant. When one half is complete, move the guide to the edge of the playing surface.

6

7

Attach dividers. When the playing surface is complete, attach the dividers and the storage tiles and corners. Allow the glue to dry overnight.

Sand the board. After the glue dries, sand the playing surface to get the surface smooth and level. Fill in any cracks with wood putty, then sand to 220 grit.

Part 2: Shelves and Frame

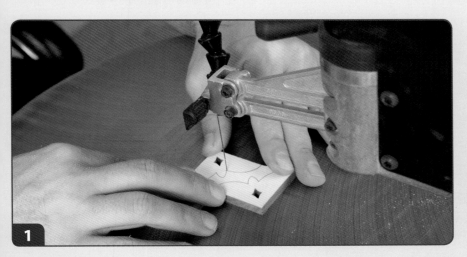

1

Cut the braces. Cut the shelf braces according to the pattern. There will be a total of 40 braces. Sixteen of the braces are laminated, so create a laminated board to cut the braces from. Use three pieces of ¼" x 4" x 12" (6mm x 102mm x 305mm) wood, two dark and one light. Glue them together with the light piece in the middle. Also cut 24 single thickness braces.

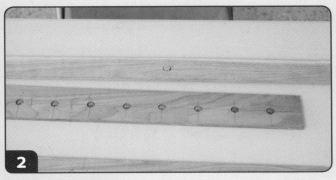

2

3

Cut the shelf pieces. Cut the shelves according to the materials list. Select eight pieces to be the top halves of the shelves and mark the centerline and the drill locations for the magnets. Drill ³⁄₃₂" (2.5mm)-deep holes with a ⁷⁄₁₆" (11mm) Forstner bit. Glue a magnet into a scrap as a guide. This will be used to keep the polarity of the magnets in the shelves consistent.

Attach magnets. Put a liberal amount of cyanoacrylate glue into each of the holes. Use the magnet jig built in the previous step to put the magnets into the shelf. This ensures the polarity of each magnet is consistent, and the magnet is pulled deep into the hole. Once all the magnets are in place, use CA activator to freeze them in place.

4

Apply putty. Fill in the holes with wood putty to ensure the magnets cannot move at all.

5

Glue the shelves together. Using a liberal amount of wood glue, glue the top and bottom halves of each shelf together and clamp. Align the centerlines for the top and bottom halves of each shelf. Allow the shelves to dry overnight. *Note: The bottom shelf doubles as part of the frame. The bottom of the shelf is ¾" (19mm) deeper than the top. Be sure to align on the front of the shelf/frame.*

6

Rout the shelves. Use the ¼" (6mm)-radius Roman ogee router bit to dress the front of the seven interior shelves.

7

Cut the dadoes. Using either a router or a table saw, cut a ¼" x ¾" (6mm x 19mm) dado into the inside back of the three remaining pieces for the frame. Use a router and a ¼" (6mm) round-over bit to dress the outside of the front and back edges.

8

Miter the corners. Use a miter saw to miter the corners of the frame. Carefully fit the frame to the board.

9

Use wood glue and brads to attach the frame to the board.

10

Attach the shelves. Align the centerline of the shelves with the center of the playing surface. Mark the edges of the shelves using a combination square and a pencil. Cut the ends off with a miter saw to get an accurate flush cut. Glue the shelves onto the board using wood glue.

11

Use CA glue to glue the crowns to each corner.

12

Attach braces. Place the laminated braces under the shelf, aligned with the center of the divider strip on each side of the playing surface. Carefully glue these braces with CA glue. The ¼" (6mm) dividers are placed along the center of the playing surface and along the frame edge with CA glue.

Part 3: Crown Flourish and Coats of Arms

1

Create the blanks for the coats of arms. Glue the wood blanks together for the large coat of arms, and if necessary, the smaller ones.

2

Create the blank for the flourish. Glue together the blank for the crown flourish. Use the two halves of the chessboard jig to provide a stable platform to glue the separate pieces together.

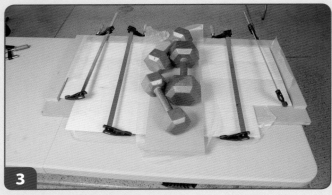

3 Keep the glue-ups flat. Clamp the crown flourish blank together securely and allow to dry overnight. Note that keeping the boards flat is a concern when gluing thin boards. I use a piece of MDF and weight to keep the boards flat.

4 Sand the blanks. When a blank is dry, sand both front and back smooth.

5 Apply tape. Apply blue painter's tape to the front of the crown flourish blank, the side flourishes, and the coats of arms blanks.

6 Attach patterns. Use spray adhesive to attach the patterns to the blanks for the crown flourish, side flourishes, and the coats of arms. The crown flourish is too large to cut in one single piece, so use the dotted lines behind the large coat of arms to cut the crown flourish into three pieces.

7 Cut the fretwork for the crown and side flourishes.

8 Cut the fretwork for the coats of arms and the backing boards. The resulting pieces are fragile, so be careful. Keep the interior pieces of the main coat of arms.

9

Glue the coats of arms to the backing boards. Glue the individual coats of arms to the backing boards. The large coat of arms has interior pieces that must be carefully fit and glued with CA glue.

10

Glue the flourish together. Glue the crown flourish back together and keep the pieces together using blue painter's tape.

11

Glue the coats of arms. Glue the coats of arms to the crown flourish using CA glue. See the picture above for placement of the coats of arms.

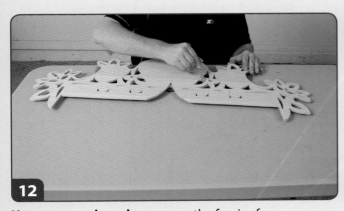

12

Use an emery board to remove the fuzzies from the fretwork.

13

Place the supports. Attach two supports to the back of the board. Locate the supports 2½" (64mm) from the edge, and have 1½" (38mm) above the top of the board frame.

14

Attach the supports. Drill three holes and countersink three #8 x ¾" (19mm) wood screws to attach the supports to the backing. I also suggest using wood glue.

15

Glue the flourishes. Use a liberal amount of wood glue on the front of the supports and glue the crown flourish to the board. Attach the bottom flourishes to the bottom corners of the board using CA glue.

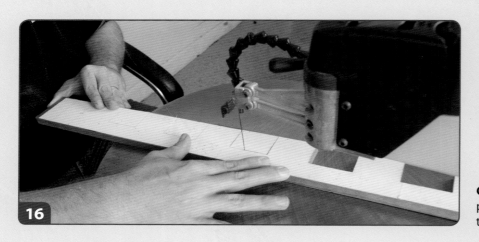

16

Cut out the crenellations. Follow the pattern for the crenellations and cut that board with the scroll saw.

17

Attach the crenellations. Glue the crenellations to the crown flourish and center the low parts with the cutouts in the flourish. Use spray polyurethane to finish the board. Use several thin coats on both the front and the back of the board.

18

Hang the board. Use two wires attached to ¾" (19mm) eye screws to hang the board. Each wire should be supported by a 50-pound rated wall hanger.

Part 4: Chess Pieces

1

Prepare the stock. This chess set uses the typical 1½" x 1½" (38mm x 38mm) stock. Size the stock, and apply blue painter's tape and the pattern as described in the section on building the Classic Chess Set (page 25). When the patterns are attached, separate the pieces using the scroll saw or a miter saw. Drill holes for the inside cuts.

2

Prepare the drill. A magnet will be placed in the base of each piece, but you should drill the holes before the pieces are cut out. Mark a 5⁄16" (8mm) depth on a ¼" (6mm) brad point drill bit.

3

Drill the magnet holes and cut the pieces. Locate the center of the base of each piece by drawing a line between the corners. Drill a hole to the indicated depth marked in the previous step. Then cut the pieces using the compound cutting jig.

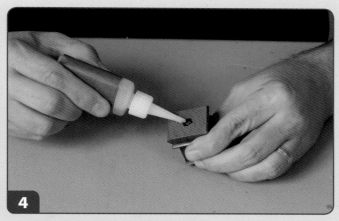

4

Insert magnets and finish. Check the polarity of the magnet so that the piece is attracted to and not repelled from the magnets in the shelves. Insert the ¼" x ¼" (6mm x 6mm) cylinder magnet into the hole and secure with CA glue. Finish with spray polyurethane and add the felt bottom.

Classic Chess Set

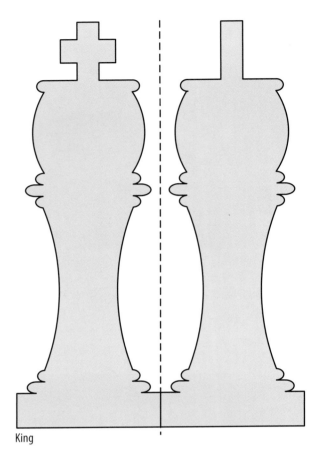

King

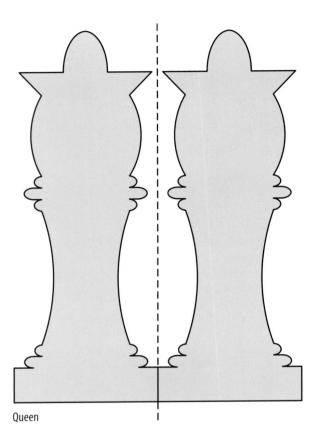

Queen

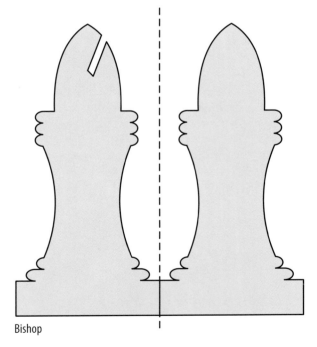

Bishop

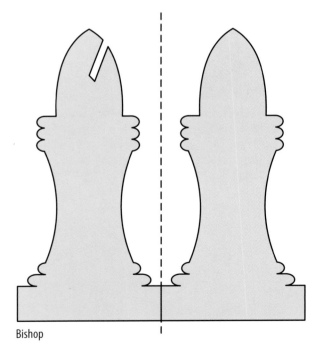

Bishop

90

Classic Chess Set *(continued)*

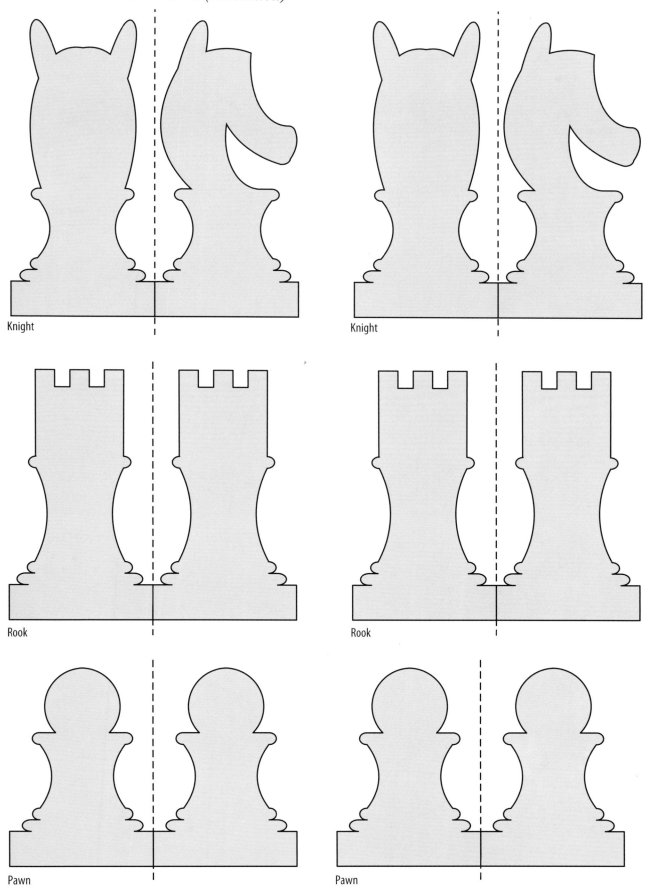

Knight

Knight

Rook

Rook

Pawn

Pawn

Pattern Appendix

Classic Chess Set *(continued)*

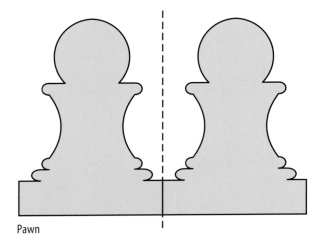

Pawn

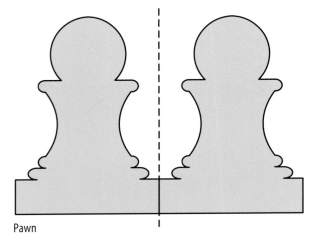

Pawn

Pawn

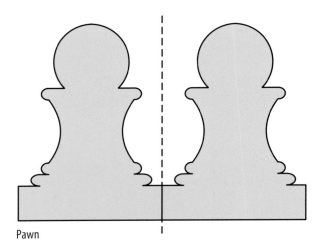

Pawn

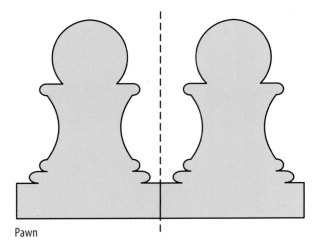

Pawn

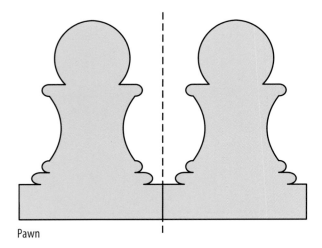

Pawn

Neo-Classic Chess Set

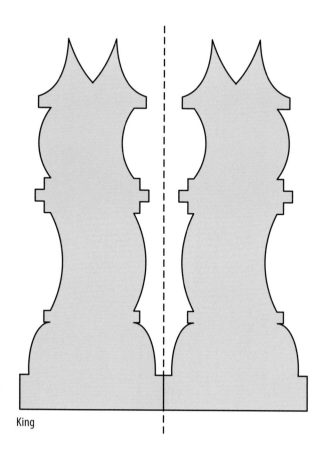

King

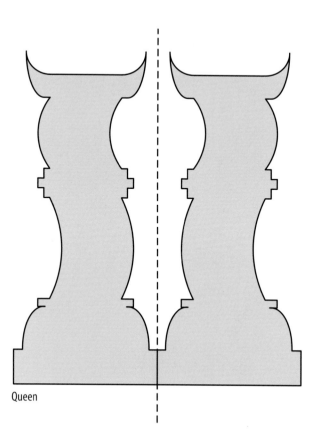

Queen

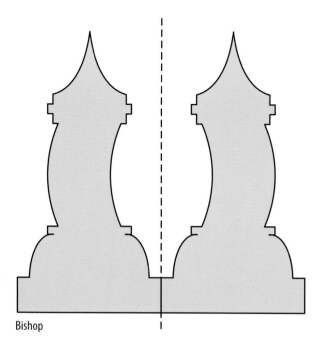

Bishop

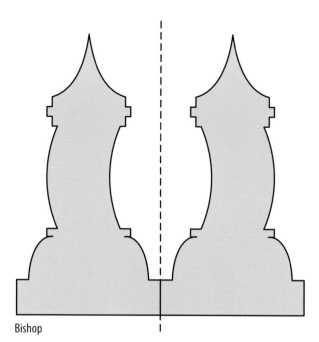

Bishop

Neo-Classic Chess Set *(continued)*

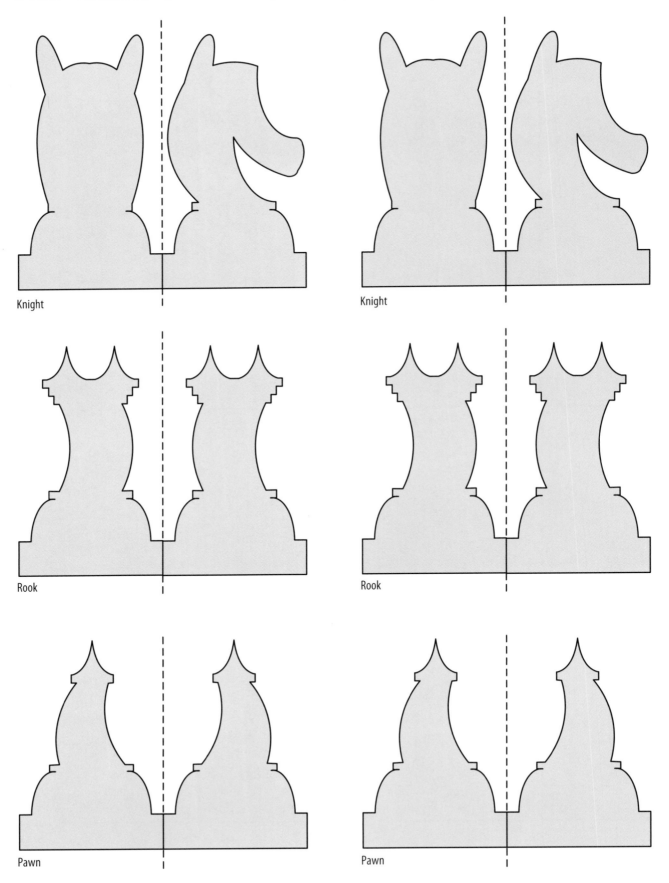

Knight

Knight

Rook

Rook

Pawn

Pawn

Neo-Classic Chess Set *(continued)*

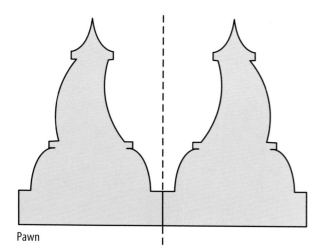

Pawn

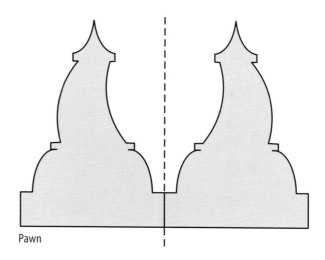

Pawn

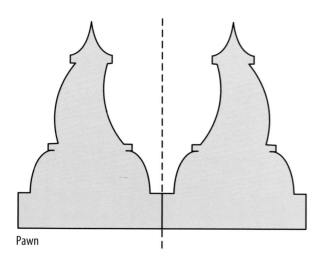

Pawn

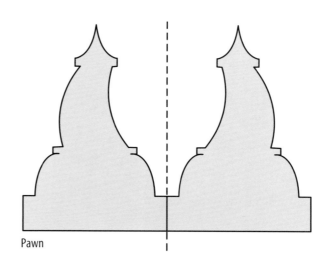

Pawn

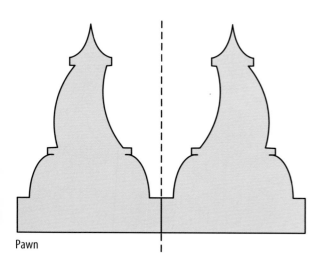

Pawn

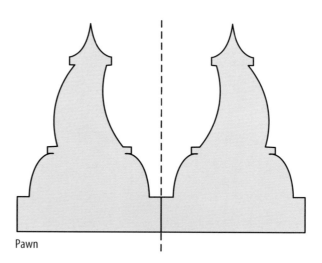

Pawn

Neo-Classic II Chess Set

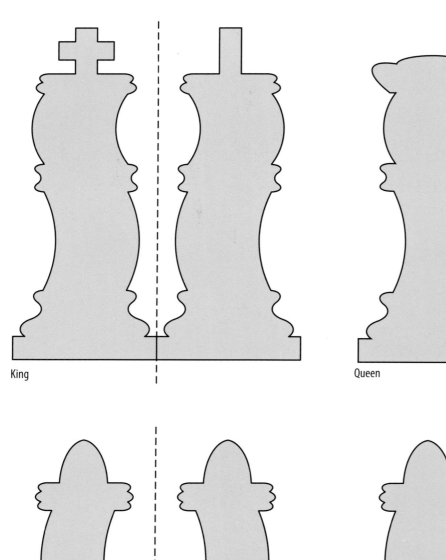

King

Queen

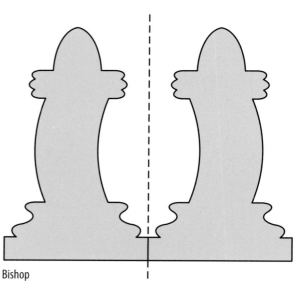

Bishop

Bishop

Neo-Classic II Chess Set *(continued)*

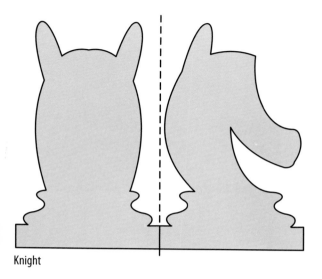

Knight

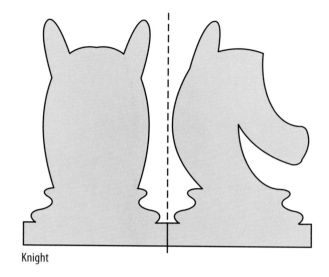

Knight

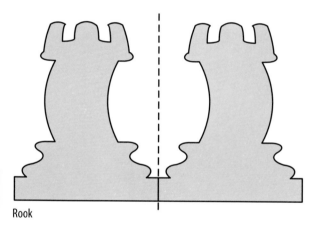

Rook

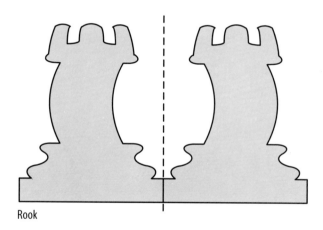

Rook

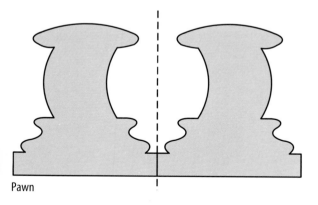

Pawn

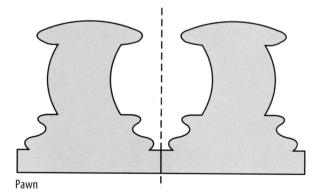

Pawn

Neo-Classic II Chess Set *(continued)*

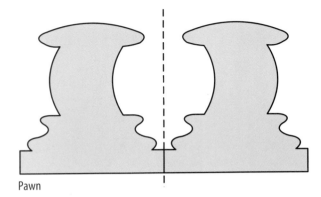

Pawn

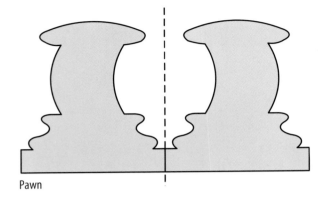

Pawn

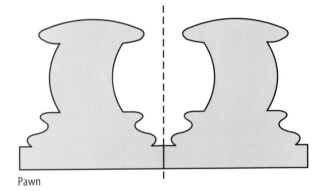

Pawn

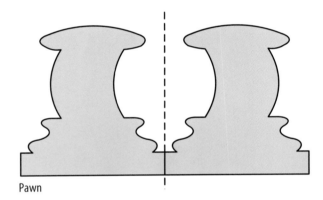

Pawn

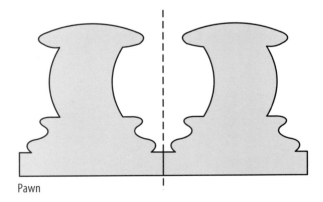

Pawn

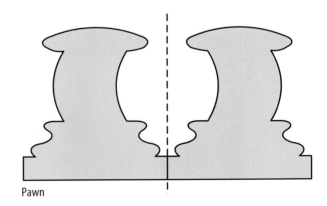

Pawn

King Henry VIII Chess Set

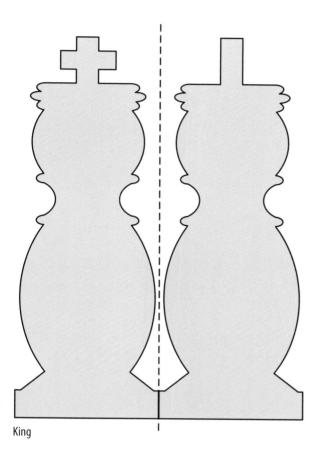

King

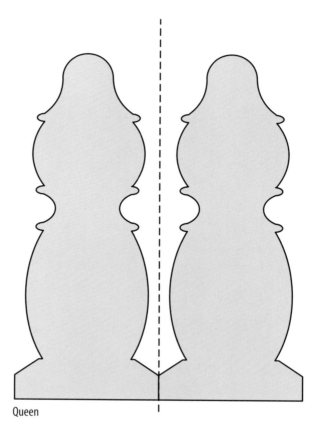

Queen

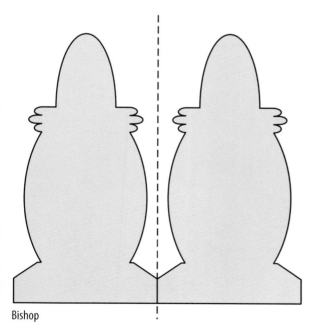

Bishop

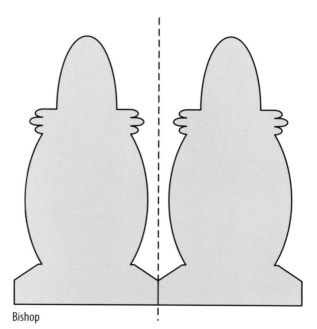

Bishop

King Henry VIII Chess Set *(continued)*

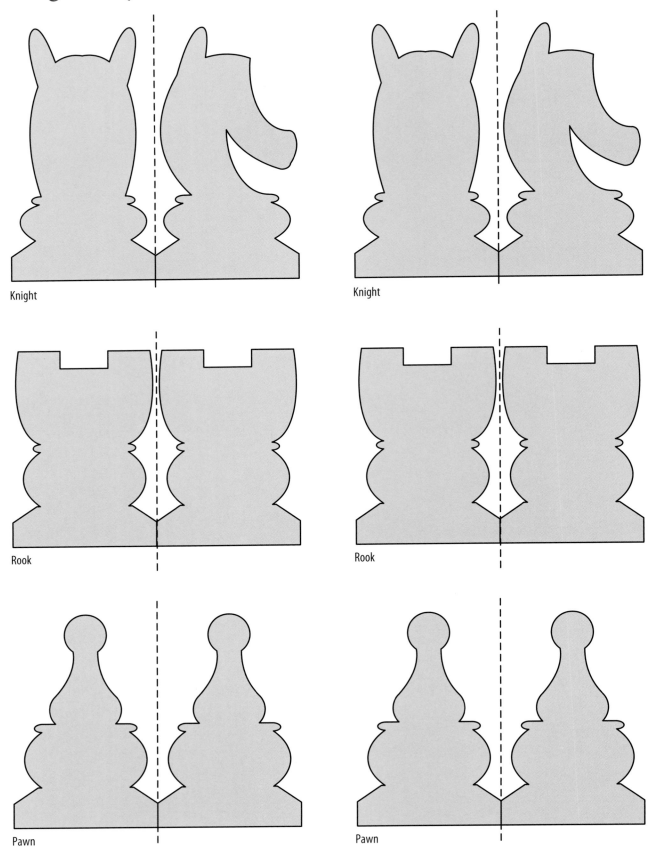

Knight

Knight

Rook

Rook

Pawn

Pawn

King Henry VIII Chess Set *(continued)*

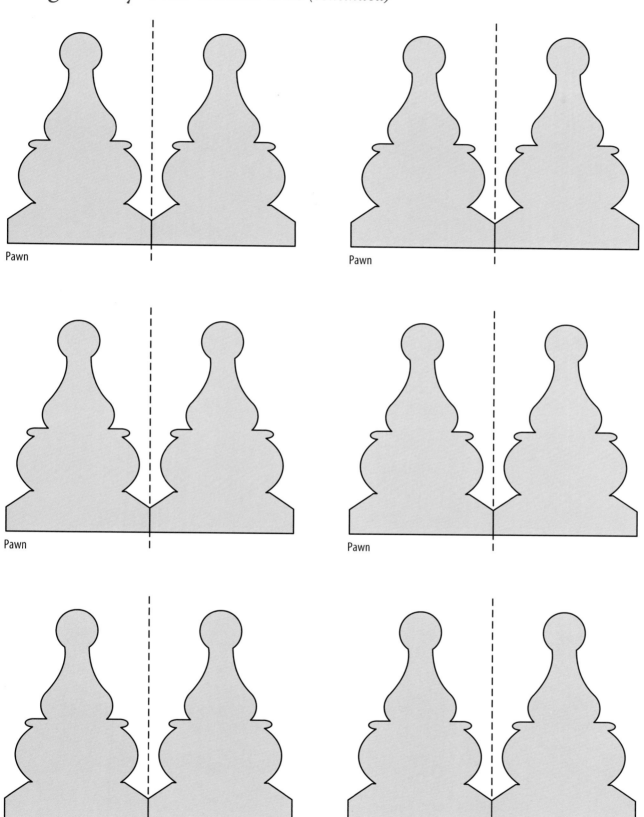

Pawn

Pawn

Pawn

Pawn

Pawn

Pawn

Trojan Chess Set

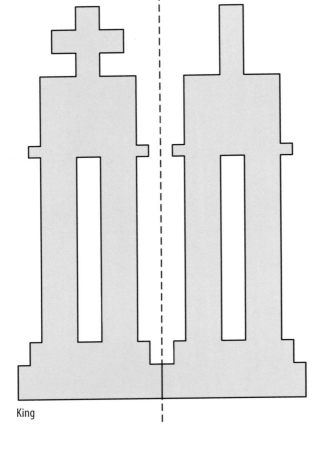

King

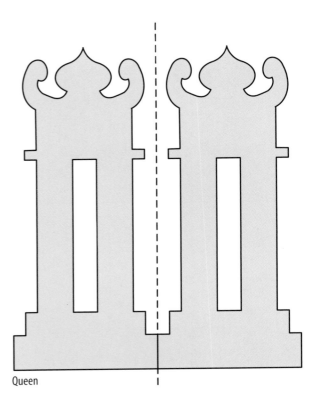

Queen

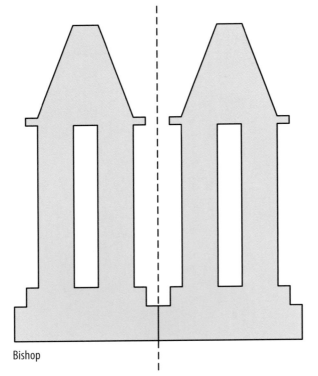

Bishop

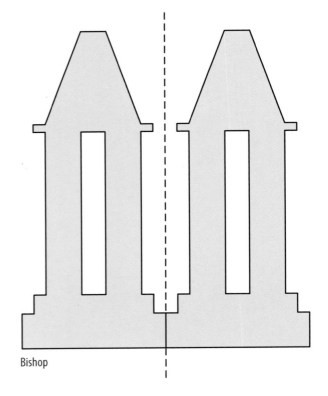

Bishop

Trojan Chess Set *(continued)*

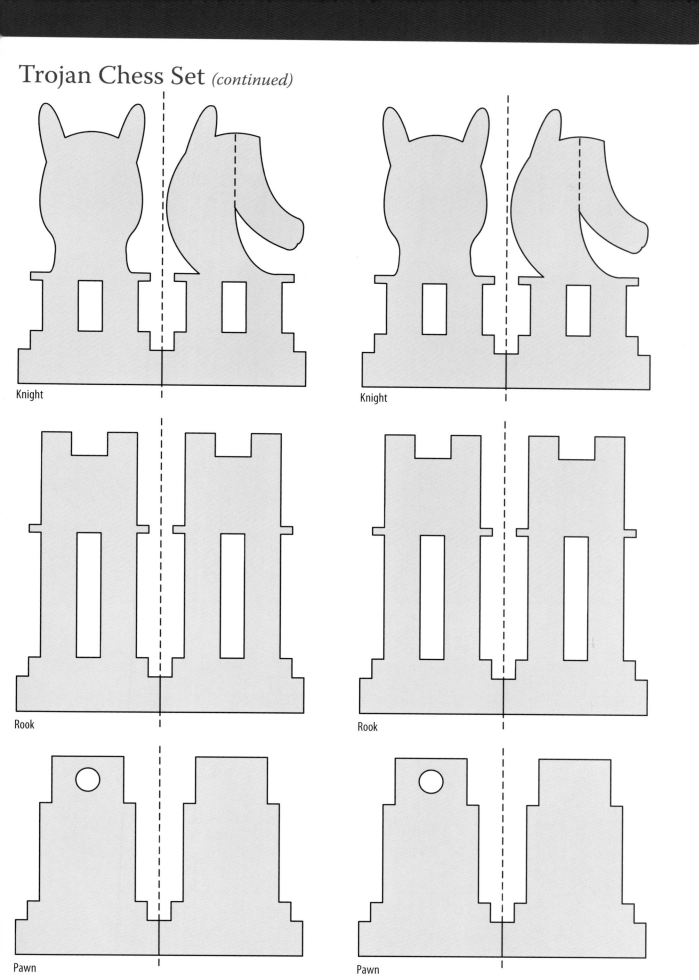

Knight

Knight

Rook

Rook

Pawn

Pawn

Trojan Chess Set *(continued)*

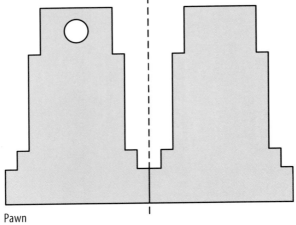

Pawn

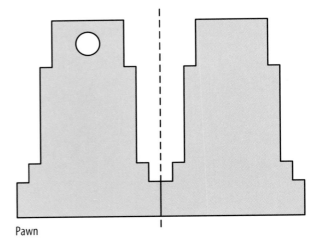

Pawn

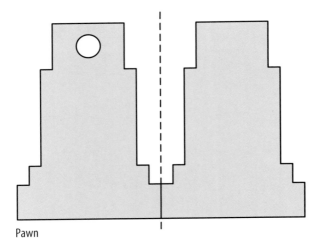

Pawn

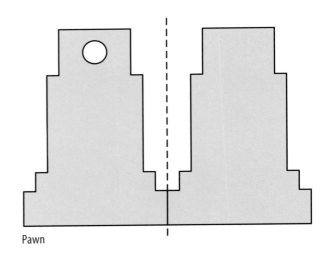

Pawn

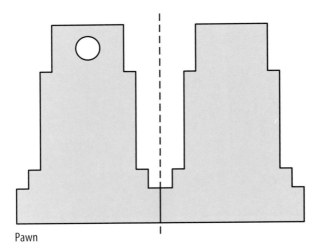

Pawn

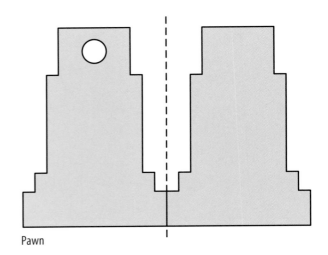

Pawn

Peter the Great Chess Set

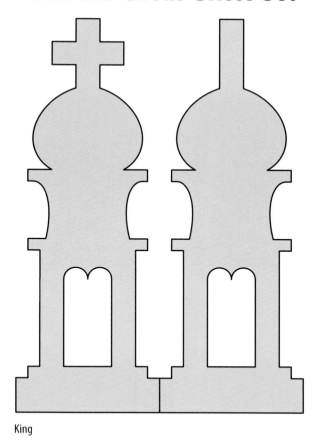

King

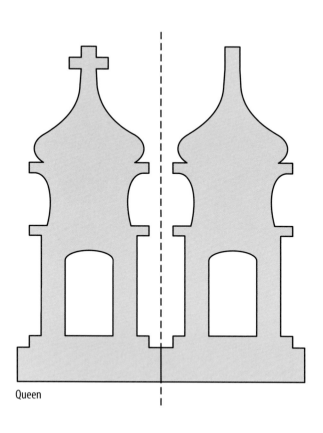

Queen

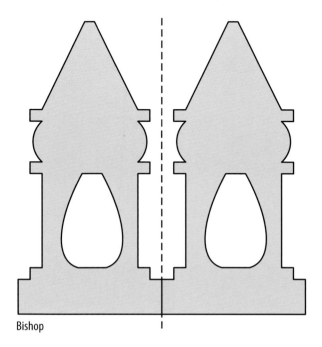

Bishop

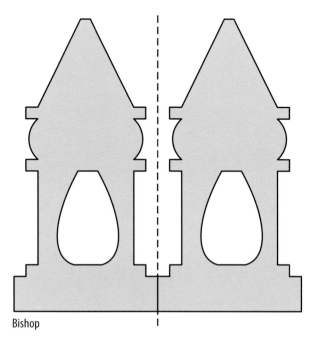

Bishop

Pattern Appendix

Peter the Great Chess Set *(continued)*

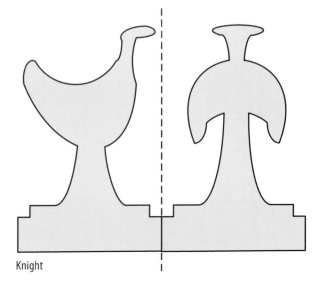

Knight

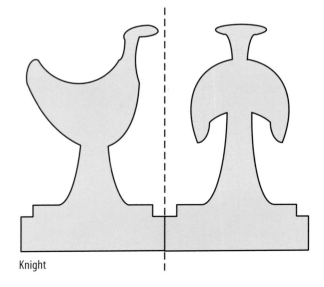

Knight

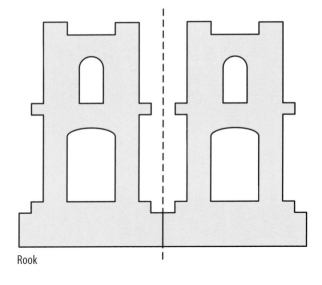

Rook

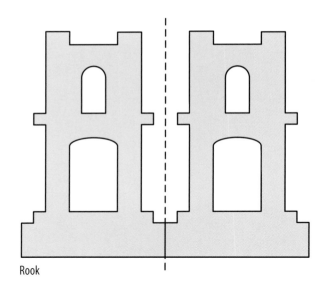

Rook

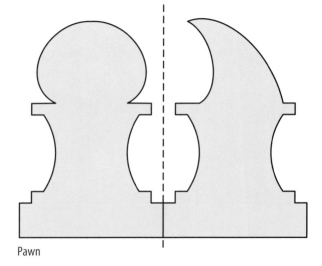

Pawn

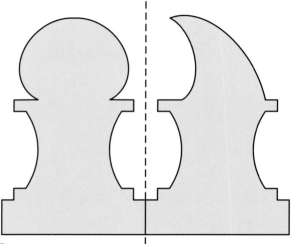

Pawn

Peter the Great Chess Set *(continued)*

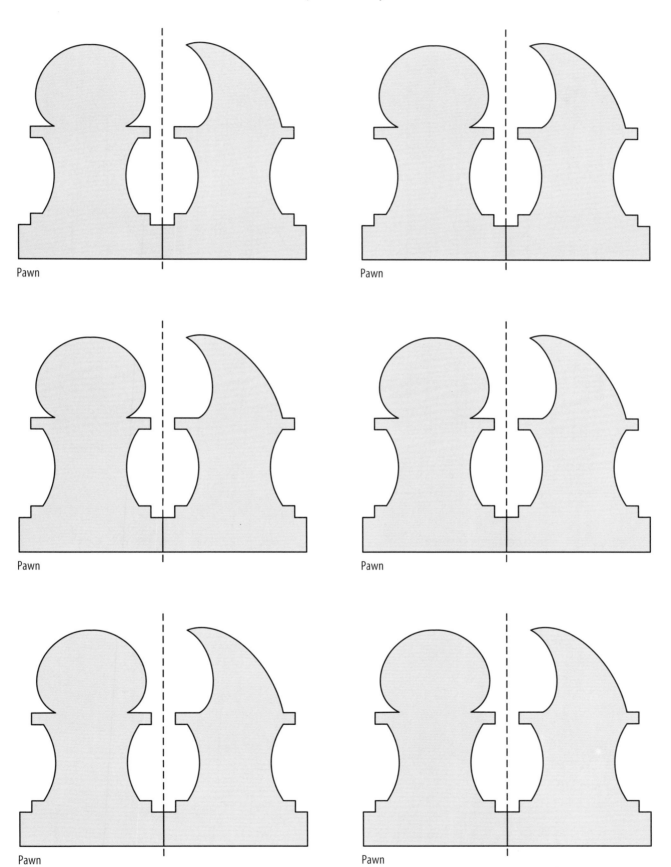

Pawn

Pawn

Pawn

Pawn

Pawn

Pawn

Canterbury Chess Set

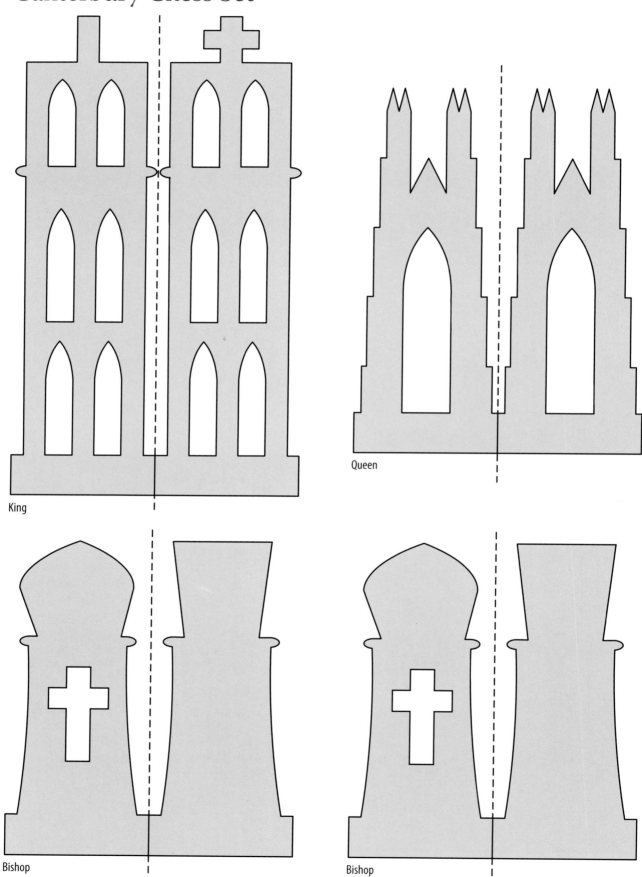

King

Queen

Bishop

Bishop

Canterbury Chess Set *(continued)*

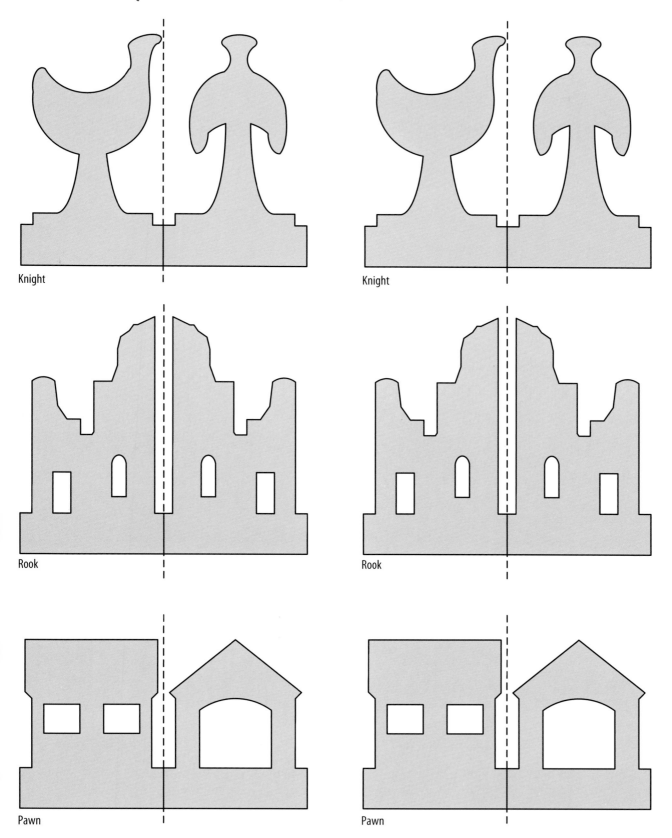

Knight

Knight

Rook

Rook

Pawn

Pawn

Canterbury Chess Set *(continued)*

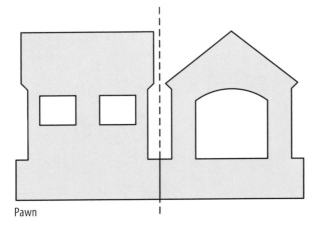

Pawn

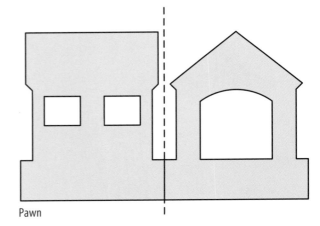

Pawn

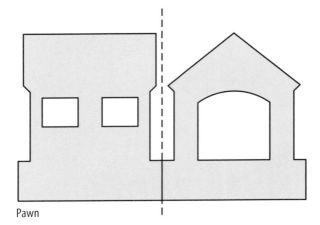

Pawn

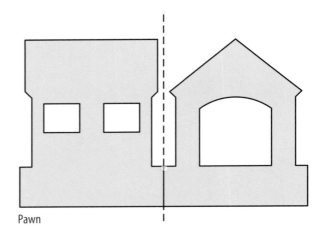

Pawn

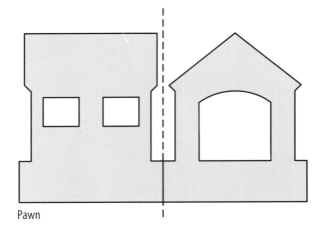

Pawn

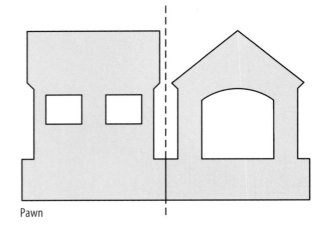

Pawn

Paris Chess Set

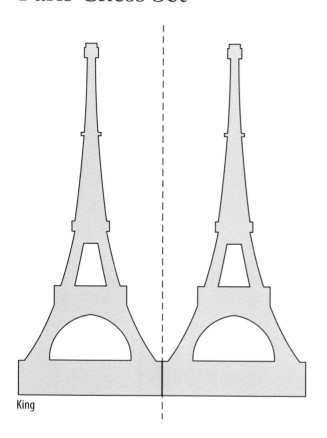

King

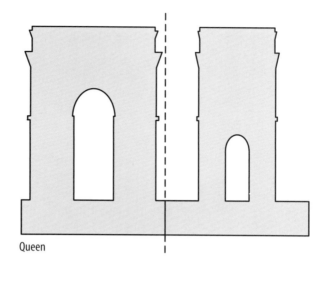

Queen

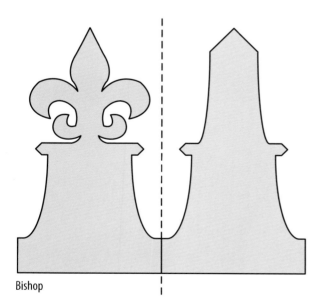

Bishop

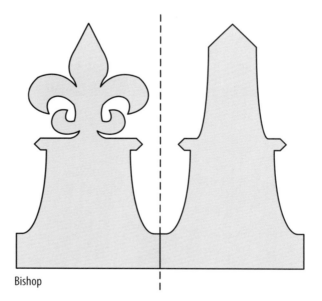

Bishop

Paris Chess Set *(continued)*

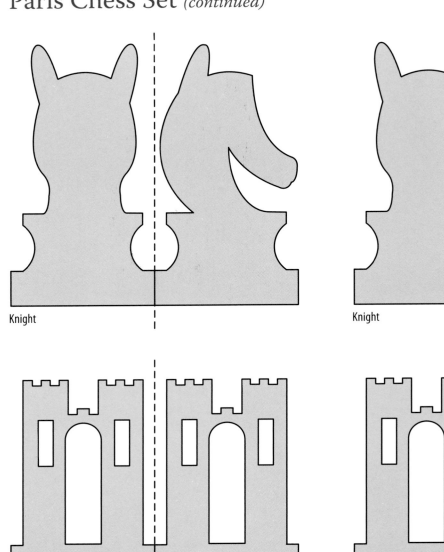

Knight

Knight

Rook

Rook

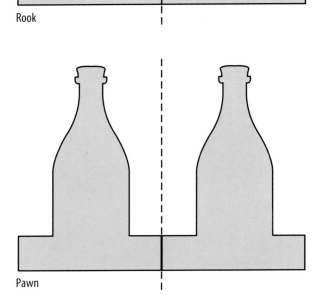

Pawn

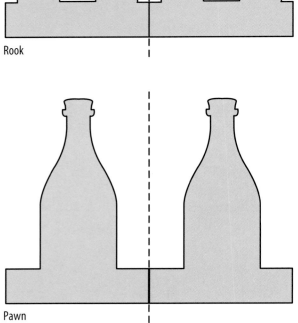

Pawn

Paris Chess Set *(continued)*

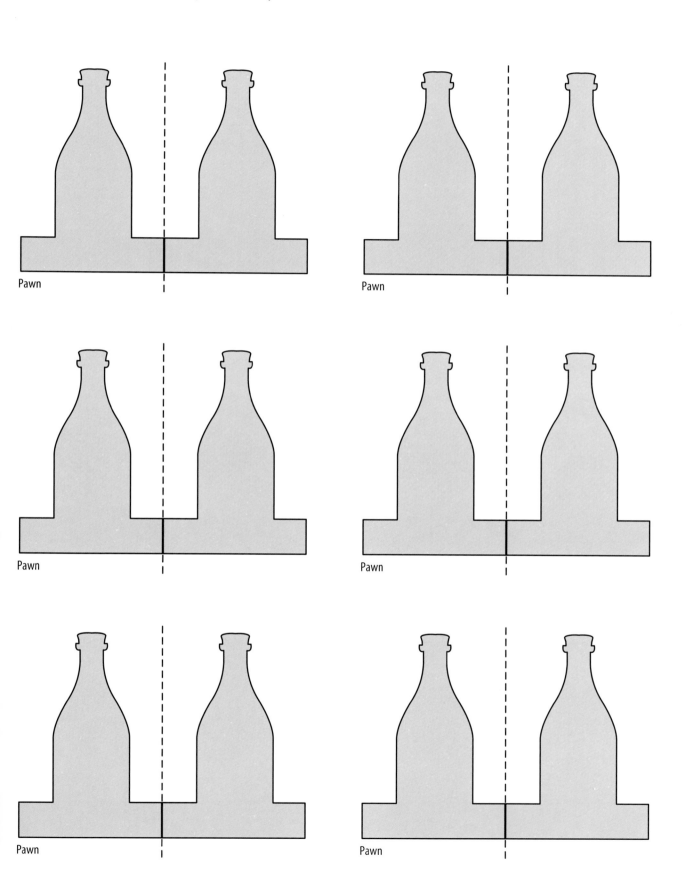

Pawn

Pawn

Pawn

Pawn

Pawn

Pawn

Roman Glory Chess Set

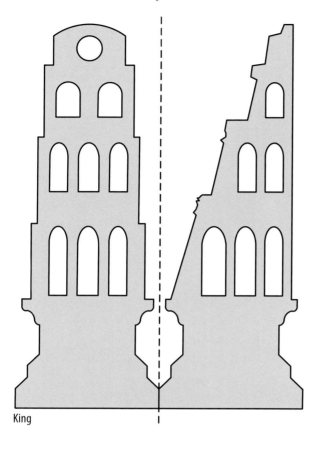

King

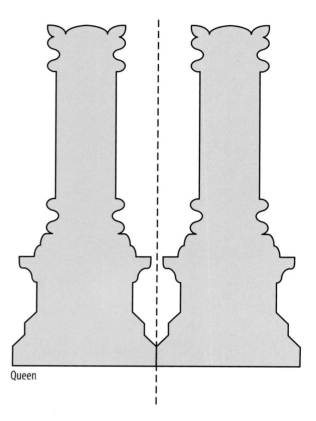

Queen

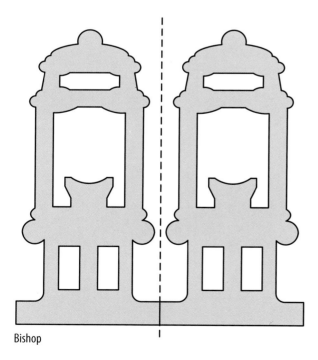

Bishop

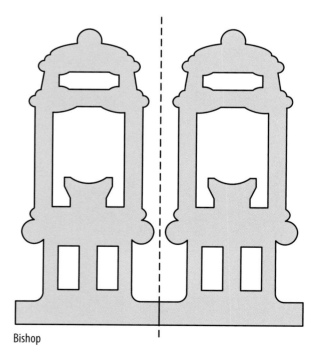

Bishop

Roman Glory Chess Set *(continued)*

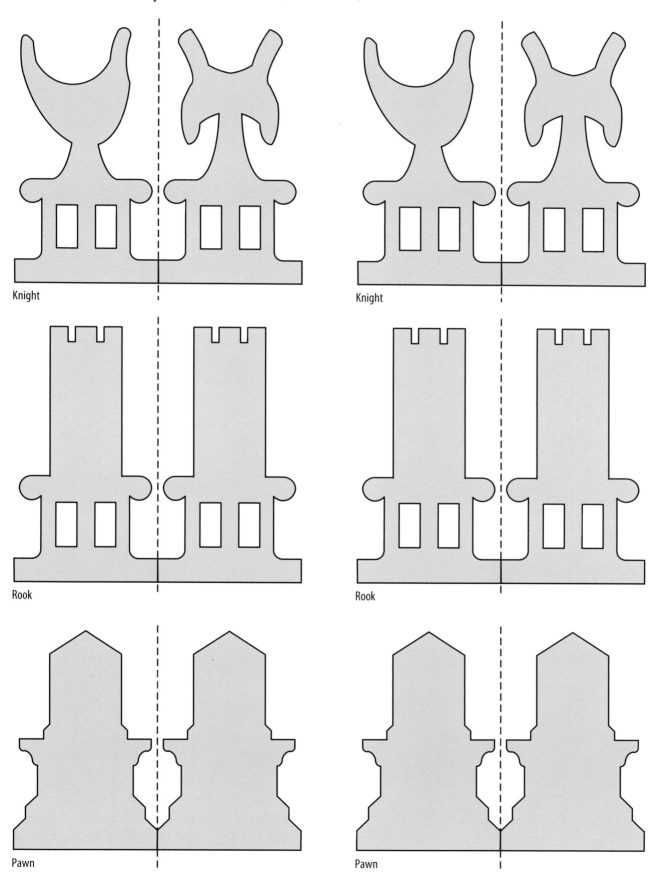

Knight

Knight

Rook

Rook

Pawn

Pawn

Roman Glory Chess Set *(continued)*

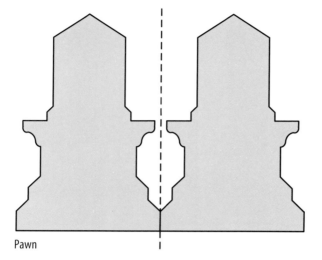

Pawn

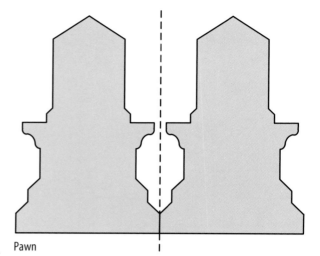

Pawn

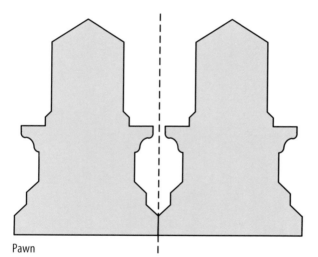

Pawn

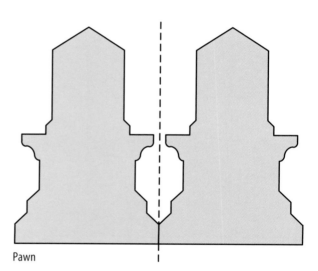

Pawn

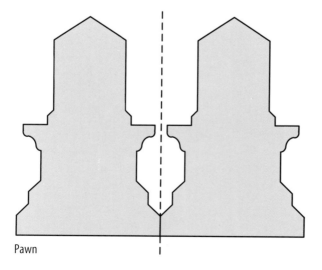

Pawn

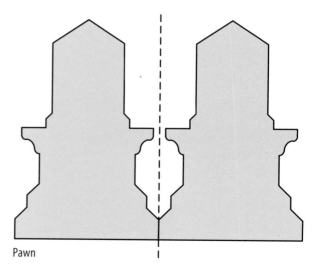

Pawn

San Francisco Chess Set

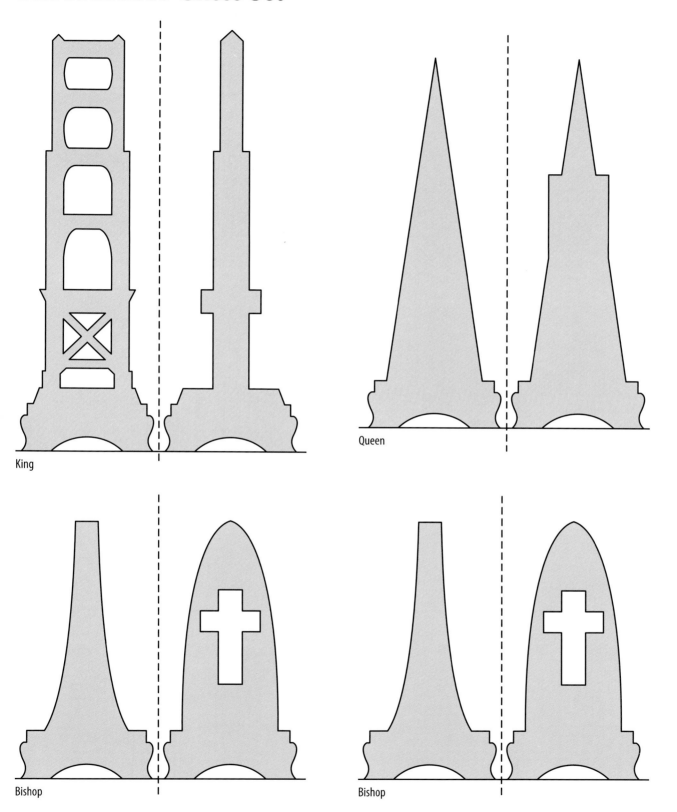

King

Queen

Bishop

Bishop

San Francisco Chess Set *(continued)*

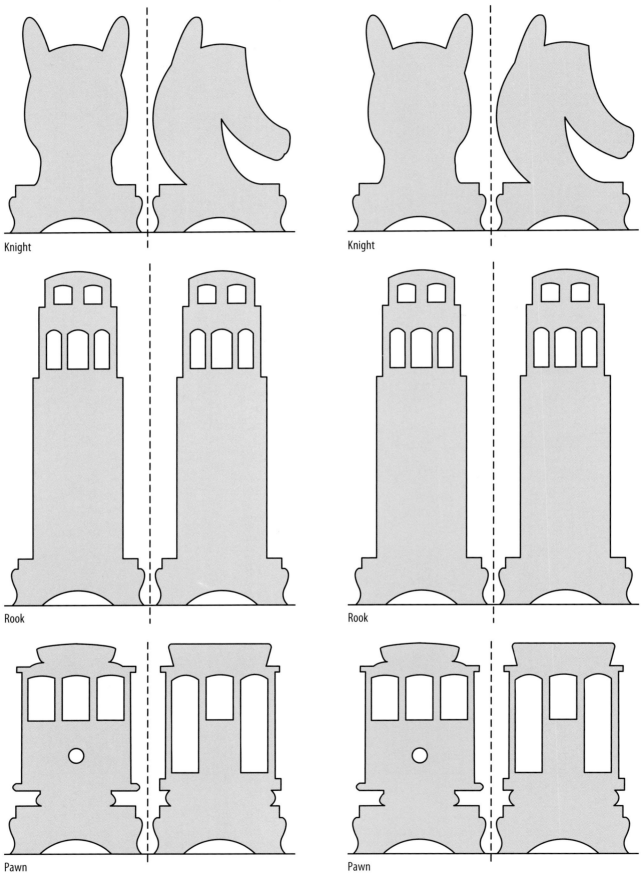

Knight

Knight

Rook

Rook

Pawn

Pawn

San Francisco Chess Set *(continued)*

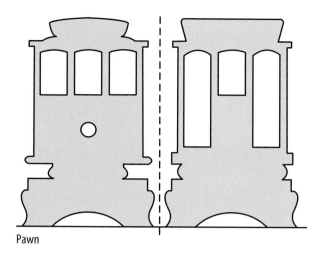

Pawn

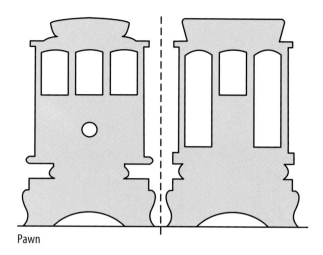

Pawn

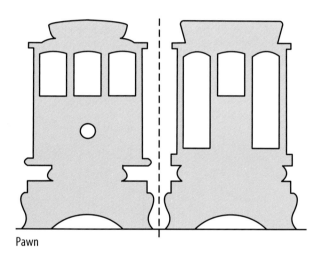

Pawn

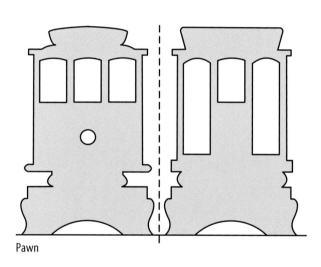

Pawn

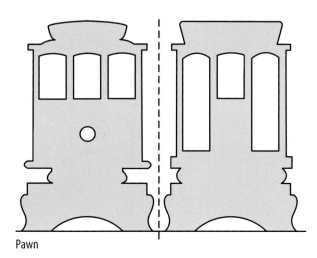

Pawn

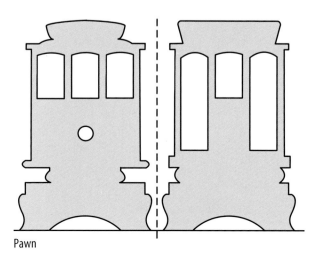

Pawn

Venice Chess Set

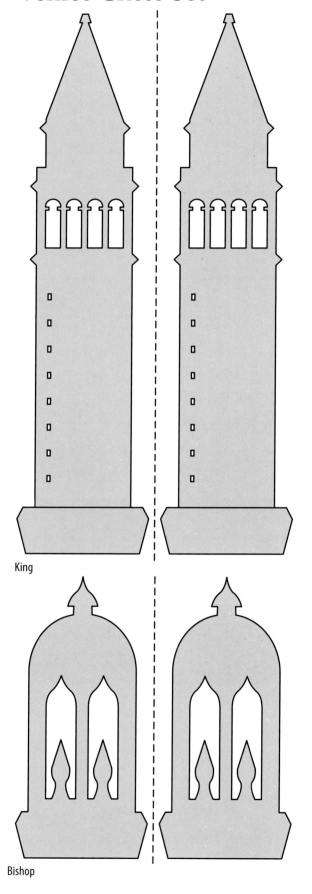

King

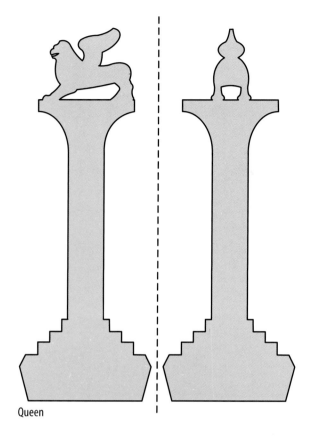

Queen

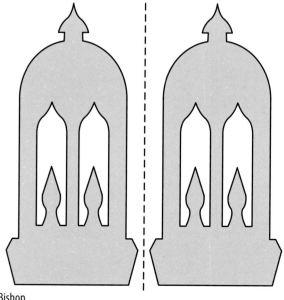

Bishop

Bishop

Making Wooden Chess Sets

Venice Chess Set *(continued)*

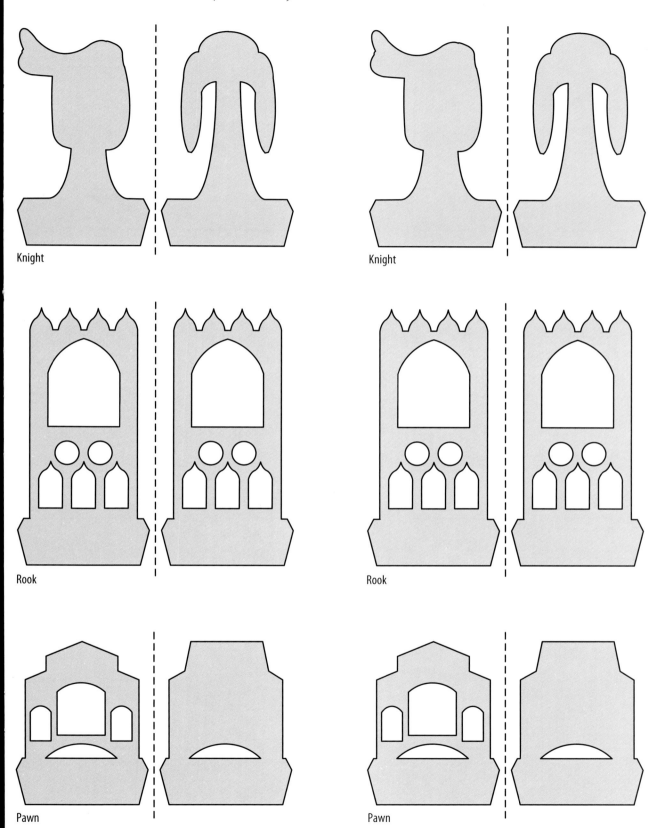

Knight

Knight

Rook

Rook

Pawn

Pawn

Venice Chess Set *(continued)*

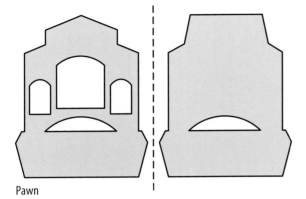

Pawn

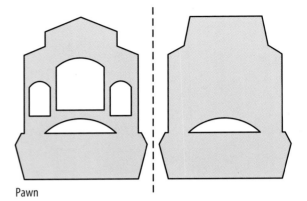

Pawn

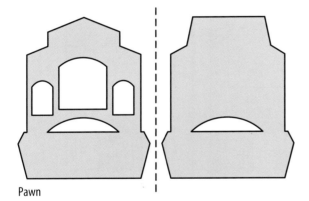

Pawn

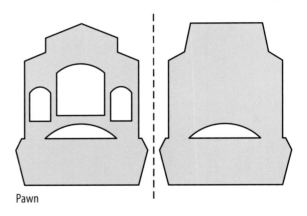

Pawn

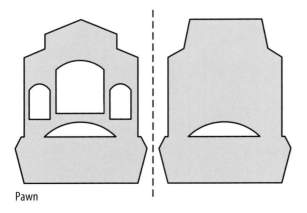

Pawn

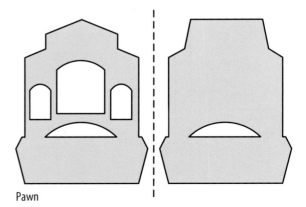

Pawn

Simple Storage Box Dividers

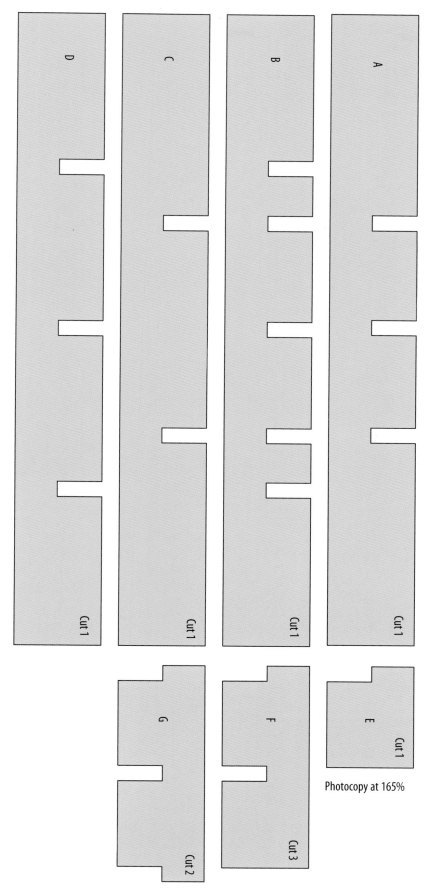

Photocopy at 165%

Travel Chess Set

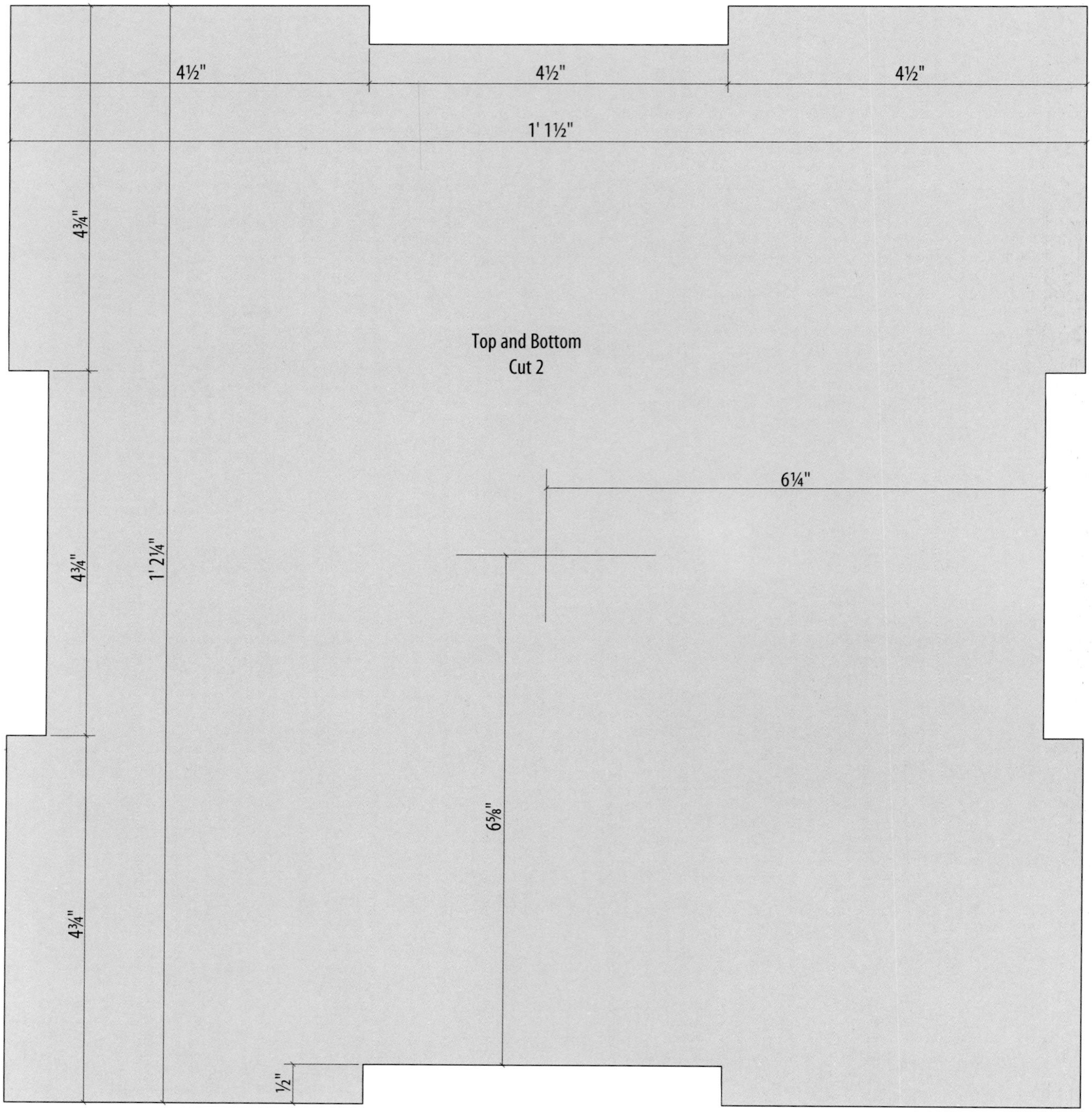

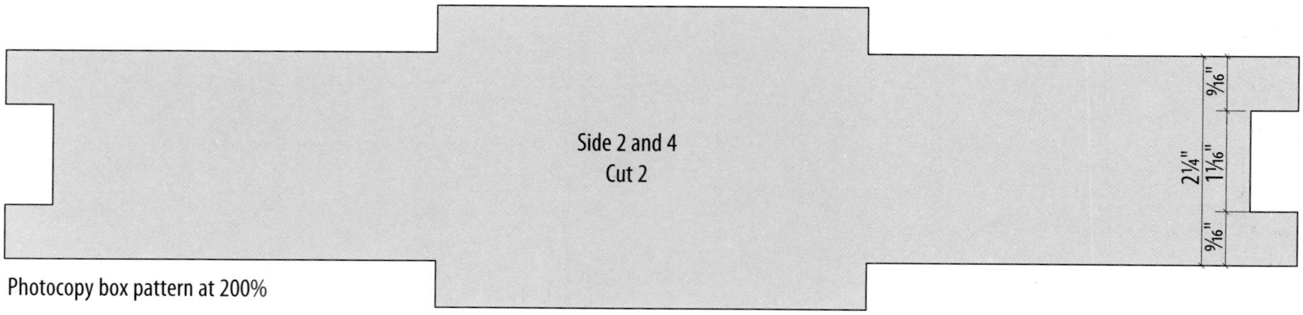

4½" 4½" 4½"

1' 1½"

4¾"

4¾"

1' 2¼"

Top and Bottom
Cut 2

6¼"

6⅝"

4¾"

½"

Side 2 and 4
Cut 2

2¼" 1¹⁄₁₆" ⁹⁄₁₆"

⁹⁄₁₆"

Photocopy box pattern at 200%

Travel Chess Set *(continued)*

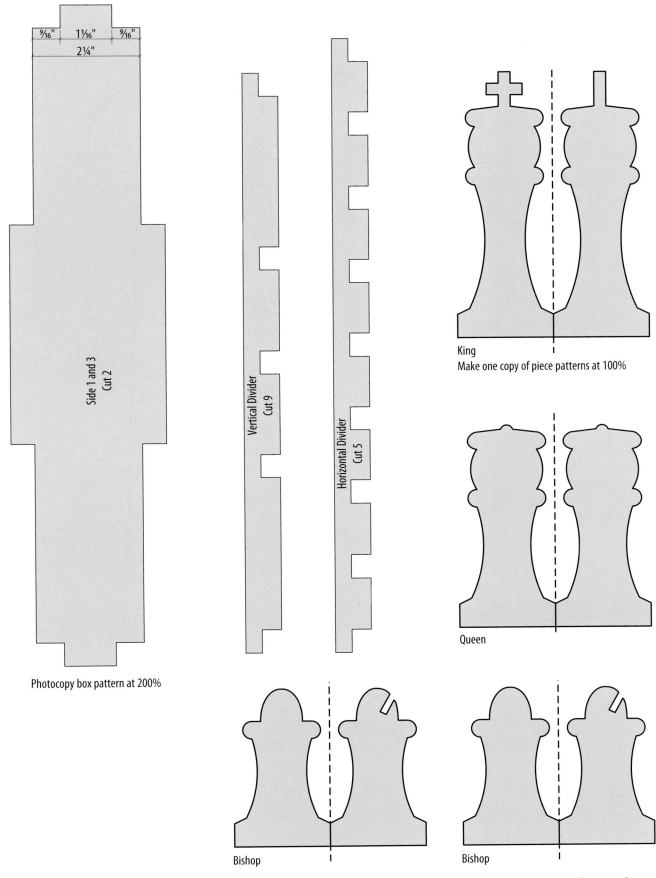

9/16"   1 1/16"   9/16"

2 1/4"

Side 1 and 3
Cut 2

Photocopy box pattern at 200%

Vertical Divider
Cut 9

Horizontal Divider
Cut 5

King
Make one copy of piece patterns at 100%

Queen

Bishop

Bishop

Travel Chess Set (continued)

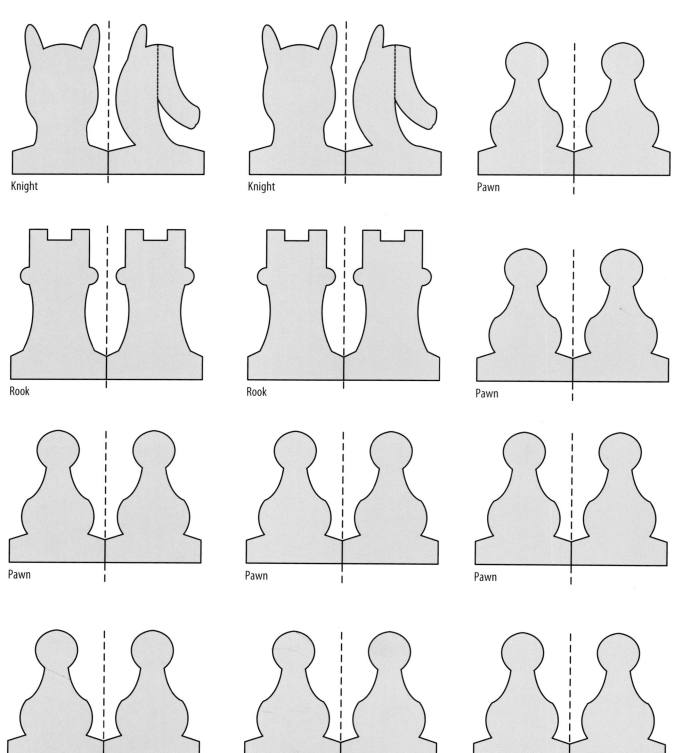

Knight

Knight

Pawn

Rook

Rook

Pawn

Pawn

Pawn

Pawn

Pawn

Pawn

Pawn

1" Jig

Photocopy at 100%

Compound-cutting jig

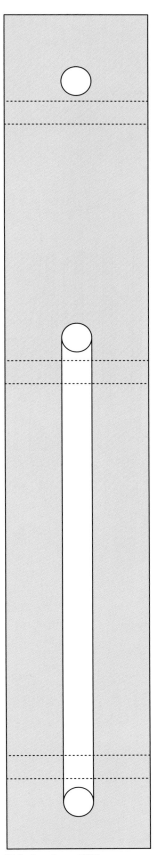

Make 2 copies at 100%

Pattern Appendix

Vertical Chess Set

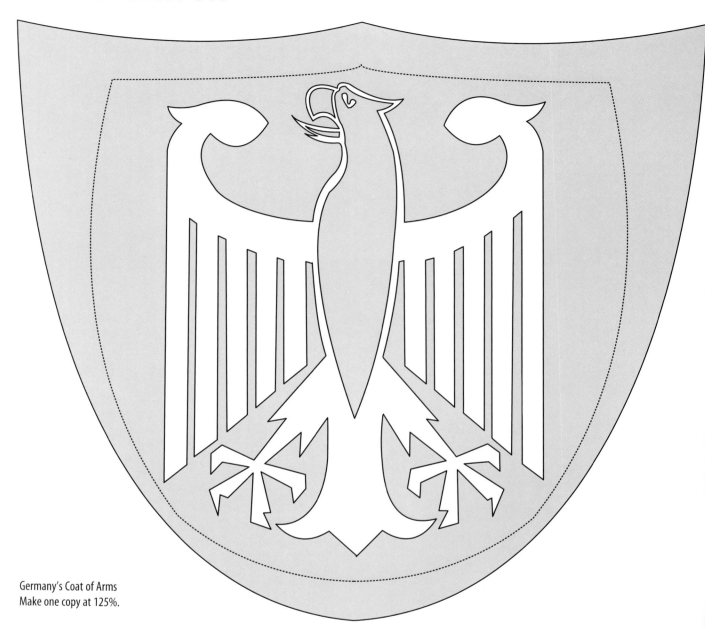

Germany's Coat of Arms
Make one copy at 125%.

Vertical Chess Set *(continued)*

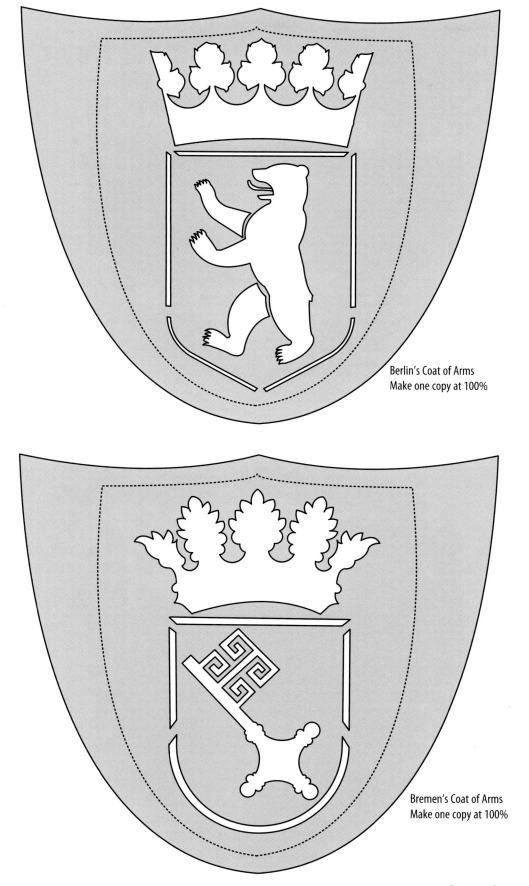

Berlin's Coat of Arms
Make one copy at 100%

Bremen's Coat of Arms
Make one copy at 100%

Vertical Chess Set *(continued)*

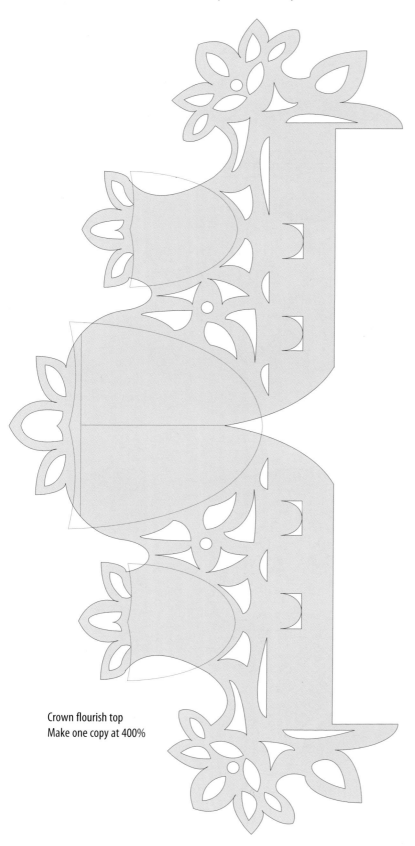

Crown flourish top
Make one copy at 400%

Vertical Chess Set *(continued)*

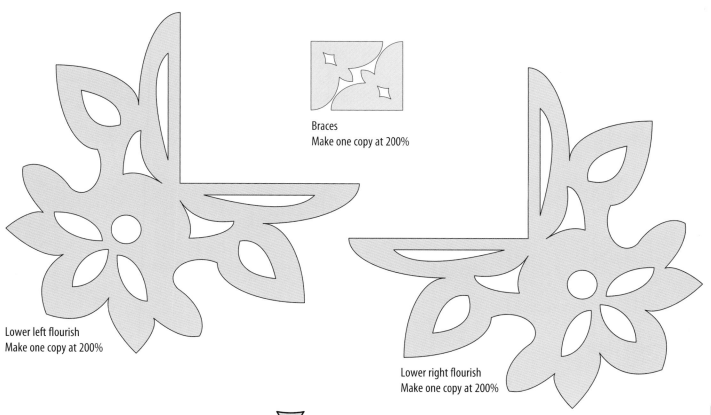

Braces
Make one copy at 200%

Lower left flourish
Make one copy at 200%

Lower right flourish
Make one copy at 200%

Crowns
Make one copy at 100%

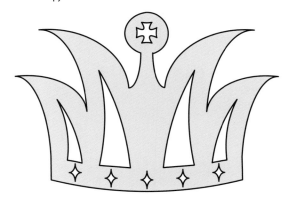

Vertical Chess Set *(continued)*

26"

2½"

Crenellations
Make one copy at 300%

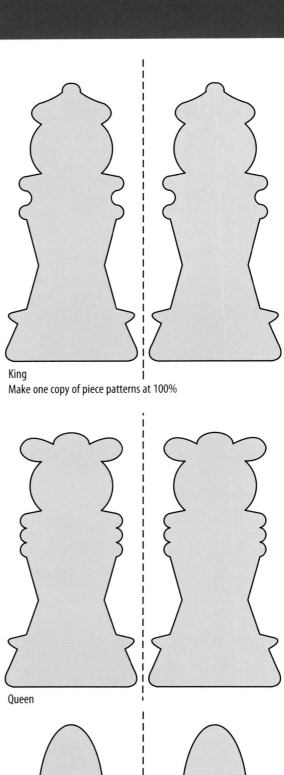

King
Make one copy of piece patterns at 100%

Queen

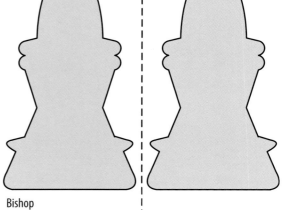

Bishop

Vertical Chess Set *(continued)*

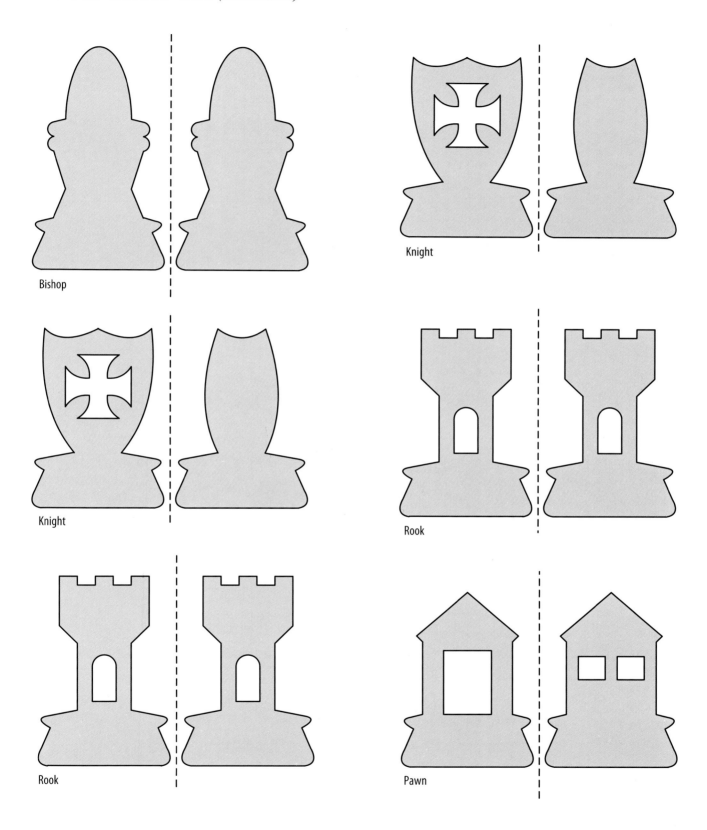

Bishop

Knight

Knight

Rook

Rook

Pawn

Vertical Chess Set *(continued)*

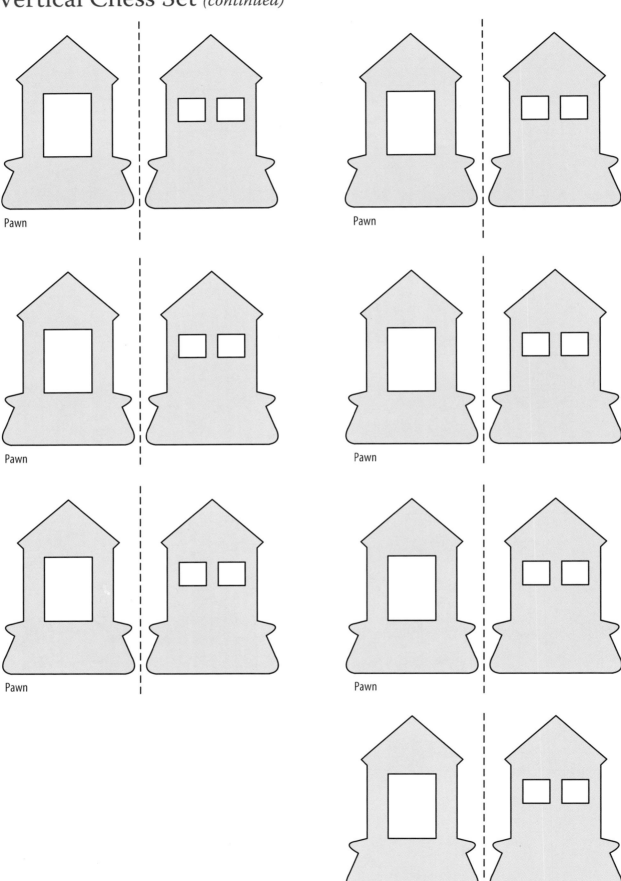

Pawn

Pawn

134

Pawn

Pawn

Pawn

Pawn

Pawn

Index

Note: Page numbers in **bold** indicate projects, and page numbers in *italics* indicate templates.

135

ACQUISITION EDITOR
Peg Couch

COPY EDITORS
Paul Hambke and Heather Stauffer

COVER AND LAYOUT DESIGNER
Lindsay Hess

COVER PHOTOGRAPHER
Scott Kriner

EDITOR
Kerri Landis

INDEXER
Jay Kreider

PROOFREADER
Lynda Jo Runkle

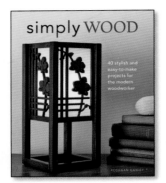
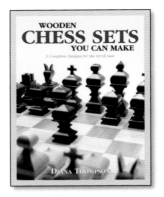
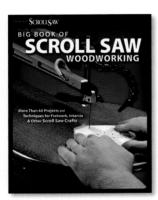
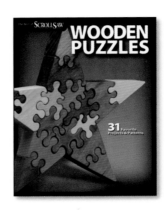
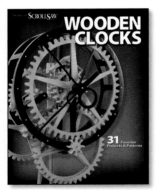
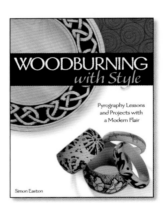